O. Sabden, A. Ashirov

D1536998

The conceptual strategy for Humankind's survival in the XXI century and food security

www.frontiercollege.ca
This book is brought to you by
Frontier College
and our generous supporters

Frontier College

Collège Frontière

Ce livre vous est gracieusement
présenté par Collège Frontière
et ses généréux donateurs

www.collegefrontiere.ca

CAMBRIDGE INTERNATIONAL PRESS

2016

Published in United Kingdom
Cambridge International Press
Imprint of: Hertfordshire Press Ltd © 2016
9 Cherry Bank, Chapel Street
Hemel Hempstead, Herts.
HP2 5DE, United Kingdom

e-mail: publisher@hertfordshirepress.com
www.hertfordshirepress.com

The conceptual strategy for Humankind's survival
in the XXI century and food security
O. Sabden, A. Ashirov ©

English

Edited by David Parry
Typeset by Allwell Solutions
Cover by Aleksandra Vlasova

---

*All rights reserved. No part of this book may be reprinted or reproduced
or utilised in any form or by any electronic, mechanical, or other means,
now known or hereafter invented, including photocopying and recording,
or in any information storage or retrieval system, without permission in
writing from the publishers.*

*British Library Catalogue in Publication Data
A catalogue record for this book is available from the British Library
Library of Congress in Publication Data
A catalogue record for this book has been requested*

ISBN 978-1-910886-26-7

Introducing Better Horizons

I suppose I wear many hats. Indeed, in the United Kingdom, I am principally known as a poet, dramaturge and critic. On the continent of Europe, however, people tend to recognise me as a Gnostic priest who perpetually reminds his congregants - without any irony - that Herbert Spencer remains one of his primary influences. With hindsight, after all, Spencer, as a Victorian progressive, claimed Knowledge-in-itself had a salvific function. In which case, he occupied a stance wherein anyone influenced by the so-called "gnostic impulse towards self-discovery" is bound to applaud. So admitted, this extremely bold intellectual assertion (daring, as it does, to imply that a paradise may be actualized on our own Earth in the manner of a scientific Garden of Eden) has continually haunted the dreams of scholars across the centuries. Assuredly, this concept of a Blessed Estate, restored through ethical tolerance, technical knowhow, and religious inspiration, still holds the vigorous promise of a secure and abundant future for us all. Each of these contentions indirectly echoing, of course, throughout Futurism as an artistic and social movement. Certainly, when one recalls that this cultural current inside industrialised societies emphasized youthful bravado, speed, technological optimism, and healthy competition, then its focus on specific objects like the Car, the Aeroplane, and the Trading City–tacitly understood as manifest icons of futurity - starts to make full sense. Along with the unbridled and heady enthusiasm of its adherents.

Without doubt, parallel "Futurist" groups in Russia, England, Italy, and elsewhere, energised notions that a better aesthetic horizon should animate our human race. A perspective empowering recent Russian literature, the visual arts and genuinely visionary sciences. Hence, the poet Vladimir Mayakovsky was a prominent member of Futurism at one point, while artists such as David Burlyuk, Mikhail Larionov and Kazimir Malevich, found endless inspiration in the imagery of Futurist writings. What is more, both poets and painters collaborated on theatrical productions like the Futurist opera *Victory Over the Sun* - with texts penned by Kruchenykh and sets built by Malevich.Unquestionably, therefore, Russian Futurists were fascinated with dynamism, meticulous research, and the restlessness of modern urban life. Perhaps their greatest error, that stated,being clearly revealed by an open repudiation of the past. An ideological fracture with historical processes never shared by those trying to build a more humane future on the received foundations of inherited social structures.

Thus, when I was asked to edit, as well as introduce, Professor O' Sabden's book, The Conceptual Strategy for Humankind's Survival in the XX1 Century and Food Security, I sensed from the outset I would be dealing with a truly unique manuscript. Overall, as a scholar whose powerful reputation goes before him, O' Sabden has already proven to be driven by insights demanding a necessary maturation in human affairs, at the very same time as demonstrating (at every step) his deepest respect for the achievements of our forebears. Obviously, I already knew he had written and lectured on a number of related topics for decades, even though the sheer passion of his work on sustainable cities, natural-resource management, automation, energy efficiency, cybernetic devices and the role of science in society, veritablytook my breath away. It is argued, nowadays, that O' Sabden advocates the type of globalization insisting on the immediate implementation of a socioeconomic system referred to as a "human-based" economy: an idea he champions with gusto, not to mention a topic he never seems to tire from thundering amid the corridors of political power.Be that as it may, even if one disagrees with his penetrating evaluation, what can one say apart from wishing him a singular "bravo" in these matters.

In terms of this essay, nonetheless, his personal analysis of the enduring significance of the Great Silk Road, the vital contribution of executive bodies, such as the United Nations, to civic advancement, along with the perceived need for financial institutions like the World Bank to effectively regulate exchange mechanisms, uncovers his unique enhancement of present-day sustainability projects. Often reminiscent of American and Russian

Futurists at their most ingenious, it can confidently be confided thatProfessor O' Sabden - as a self-confessed social engineer - fearlessly defends his view that a new dawn is finally achievable by humanity on its evolutionary march towards utopia. As such, this is an important volume marking an essential injection of renewedelation into the millenniaahead: a message of hope on a planet occasionally guilty of abject moral despair. And each a reason why, I wholeheartedly commend this uplifting text to Anglophone readers as a taster of enriching things yet to come.

David Parry
London 2016

Intro

As the third millennium dawns, this world storms and changes unpredictably. Hence, it has become difficult to calculate what to expect on the morrow. Indeed, questions of recovery from innumerable crises (along with any possible rescue plan for humankind from adverse global conditions), are now paramount. After all, dangers such as rapid climate change, water scarcity, not to mention preventable food shortages, obviously shake social stability and economic sustainability on a planetary scale. At the same time, of course, as potential resource-based political conflicts appear on the horizon, various natural cataclysms, pure accidents, and negative environmental processes are increasing. All presenting humanity with unprecedented socio-environmental issues. Each one of which has (arguably), been generated through a deliberate refusal to apply "objective" economic principles, an active interest in wildlife conservation, or for that matter any employment of tried and tested managerial laws governing cyclical unfolding.

So stated, these instances of adaptation emerged, first of all, in the consciousness of people: only thereafter configuring generally within world psychology. This is why every one of these problems demands a revival of spiritual and moral values. It is time, therefore, as every fair-minded observer can see, for our human race to bring order into its own house!

As such, this present megaproject is a scientific hypothesis for a better future for everyone. Yet, neither futurology, nor predictions, or imaginative visions, in themselves provide a full solution. Rather the emergence of a real **conceptual strategy for humankind's survival in the XXI and further centuries** is required. What is more, the rubrics behind the creation of a universal civilization are demanded: if, that is, a post-industrial world, founded on spirituality, scientific and technological innovation, ecology, space exploration and world safety, are to become realties.

Undoubtedly, considering the fact 1.3 billion people are currently starving, special attention must be paid to food security. A topic already preoccupying a number of countries present day governments. However, only systematic and coordinated measures regarding the six basic components of security can actually provide the world with a steady life in its highly diverse domains. In which case, it is telling that these theoretical breakthrough-ideas have arisen in the epicentre of Eurasia. Territories wherein alternative options to those defended by the XXI century Western world can be clearly explored in a genuinely globalized context.

With these arguments in mind, we seek to address laymen, as well as members of the UN, members of international public organizations, scientific centres, corporations and the mass media, along with anyone who is not indifferent to future human civilization.

Table of Contents

CONCEPTUAL STRATEGY FOR HUMANKIND'S SURVIVAL IN THE XXI CENTURY

CHAPTER I

The rubric behind this scientific megaproject

Empires of the future will be reasonable ones

U. CHURCHILL

The evolution of terrestrial life-forms arising billions years ago was characterized by a developmental logic in world history: **flora → fauna → mind, human society → biosphere → noosphere** etc. Unarguably, these are the main stages of living progression on our planet.

During their long fight for survival, however, human beings started studying themselves, as well as the world around them. Thus, they learned Creations laws and tried to apply these principles in a way whereby opportunities for satisfaction would increase according to humankind's requirements. Moreover, as this seven thousand year unfoldment continued, humanity preserved its experience, along with its accumulated knowledge, in order to prepare for its future destiny.

Beyond doubt, throughout history, there were many crises. Conflicts, wars and so on. Yet, there has never been such a critical situation as the one if which we find ourselves nowadays. A time when the very existence of civilization as a whole is under threat, while the problem of limited resources is fast becoming an everyday topic of discussion in scientific circles. Each subject ultimately suggesting that the preservation of human civilization (irrespective of its subsequent successful advancement), are futile fields of inquiry without studying the general regularities and proportions surrounding production, consumption, reproduction cycles, or the eventual management of global processes.

This is why it is important to develop an **integrated concept of transition to post-industrial civilization.** An assertion proved by prerequisites and conditions discovered within our world's aforementioned historical evolution. Phrased differently, a case demonstrated through the formation of logic propositions that all scientists and significant members of our world community accept, even though they examine this issue from a variety of positions [1,2,3].

So understood, it could be argued that the objective logic of the world's historical development may serve as a reference point (standard) providing the only accurate evaluation-criterion of Past, Present and Future conditions. Formulated correctly, such knowledge becomes a necessary moral compass as humanity enters into a period of global transition from an industrial to a post-industrial civilization.

Conventional efforts to overcome global challenges become less and less efficient while a failure to act promptly may lead to unpredictable and irreversible consequences, which are potentially devastating for all of humanity. Therefore, today, as never before, we must not only have a clear understanding of the causes of the unprecedented imbalance in global social-and-public development of present times, but also have a vision to solve the problem of global synthesis. In other words, we must exercise a truly science-based foresight. From these positions, the solution to our innumerable problems may be discerned through the construction of a **planetary dwelling for universal civilization** (figure 1).

All in all, informed commentators intuit an increased understanding that each nation needs to coordinate every aspect of scientific, technical, ecological, aeronautical, spiritual and economic security, as a uniform system. A structure without which the possibility of universal civilization (including a transition from the biosphere into the noosphere - not only on Earth, but also in space), cannot emerge.

As seen above, this planetary "home" of universal civilization, along with future waves in scientific and spiritual evolution, will be founded on

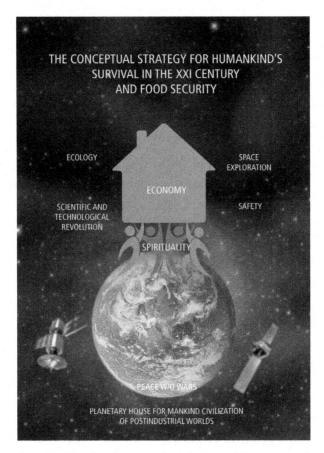

Drawing 1: Planetary home of universal civilization for a post-industrial world

a **combination of six key Basic Elements of transition** to post-industrial civilization, such, as:

1. *Humanization of the world community - taking into account the received logic of world history's previous development.*
2. *New scientific and technological innovation, technological methods (VI-VII-TW).*

3. *Ecology and stabilization of world power consumption.*
4. *Space exploration, space energy and the resources of our Solar system.*
5. *World safety.*
6. *Transition from a market economy to a "revolutionary" economy for post-industrial civilization.*

Overall, the main objective of this megaproject is to develop conceptual formulations outlining transitional models towards **post-industrial civilization. Propositions, dare one say, built on transitional components already debated in the public arena**. For example, recovered spirituality, society's humanization (defined by the logic of our world's historical development), observable scientific and technical progress, a "greening" of society and the material world (an ecological revolution), space exploration, world security and, additionally, our planets actual economic potential are already under discussion. Every one of them providing parameters provided for an increasingly steady life inside our planetary home. Unsurprisingly, if only 200 States became members of a single family, peacefully living under one cultural "roof", a uniform planetary home for universal civilization appears more or less unstoppable (see figure 1). Instructively, all six Basic Elements of civilizations "genotype" are presently undergoing a profound transition in the first quarter of our XXI century – prophesying deep changes for the better.

Yet, the radical difference of this megaproject from the research results of scientific visionaries, Nobel Prize laureates and respected scholars in physics, chemistry, medicine, physiology, literature, peace studies and economics, remains in the unified approach of its authors. Indeed, this monograph (possibly for the first time ever) tries to construct an openly unified "systems approach" to all six basic transitional components of civilization, while interconnecting spiritual and scientific processes **(figure 1)**. Stated so, our synthesis of fundamental scientific theories in the various subject-domains of knowledge, along with our **management** of the Basic Elements previously described, evolved a unique style of organizational creativity. An original "map", as it were, uniting abstract and concrete learning into a comprehensive picture portraying an emergent world civilization. Thus, each component within our general "house" of civilization is envisaged as a theoretical and actual unit. Worded differently, each one is a necessary "member" examined through the lens of fundamental sustainability - which nonetheless demands an interdisciplinary scientific appraisal in terms of known criteria, indicators etc. The creation of such a house for future civilization, however, soon falls apart if any of the six blocks are casually removed. As such, this is a tight-knit systematic idea revealing an exit strategy from global crisis to enduring advancement.

In figure 1, the "parental" house is a place where love reigns. Herein, one cares not only for oneself, but also for humankind's general welfare: for the happiness of all people on Earth, for the life-systems of our planet - based on new knowledge, spirituality, science and the foundations of Reason. At this interface, materiality and spirituality merge in human consciousness.

It needs to never be forgotten, of course, that this house of civilization would be constructed by every person alive - being built from genuine spirituality and the real development of human nature. Otherwise, the desired quality of life achieved through the performance one's empathic duties will not arise. So, for the first time, we, the authors, defend a thesis claiming that economics should neither be based on the satisfaction of material or spiritual needs regarding an abstract consumer. Rather, economics must rest **on the consumption patterns of a specific person**. Henceforth, we insist that every economic foundation must stand on wellbeing, the friendship of those around us, as well as those harmonious relations reigning between all people of goodwill. Perspectives serving to evolve future psychological peaks, instead of the current "Mammon attitude", which worships wealth for its own sake.

Attentively looking at our book cover, one notices an illustration depicting this view through examining our planet from outside – from space. After all, having rejected local continental conditions, national, along with social parameters, we felt it necessary to see our past, present and future from space. Watching everything from the vantage point of neighbouring planets in our Solar system: from the vast Galaxy itself. Perhaps, such a vision will permit a break from inherited deadlocks? Maybe, our opponents will respect the insightful imagination of the authors? Possibly, but more probably, they will merely encounter speculations. With these potential reactions in mind, we have elected to quote Einstein when he states, "problems cannot be solved on the same level whereon they arose". This is why we shamelessly claim the future will witness new technological novelties providing humanity with prosperity.

It is equally necessary to emphasize that globalization **integrates ideas**. It allows for a joint consideration (and solution) of problems in a quicker manner than previously achieved. Any assessment of a decisions efficiency will, henceforth, accord with a scientific outlook, while scientific instruments will themselves suggest solutions based on the fundamental laws of nature: principles, which don't depend on heads of state, multinational companies, Freemasonry, pan-Islamic political parties, or any other association. Instead, a **planetary collaboration between nations - along with its attendant ethnos** - will be adopted by everyone. In this way, human society will advance into a type 1. global civilization.

Understandably, some caution needs to be exercised with these reveries. A macroidea, whether desired, or not, can easily turn into "burning issue" sweeping like an avalanche across the world and blinding the eyes of humanity at large. In our plan, therefore, small strategic steps - taken one at a time - eventually mark the process of emergence. Today, world debates surrounding climate change, nuclear armament and other military operations, migration, hunger and food security are already on the political agenda. New problems, this said, like - *joint space exploration, the preparation for VII technological ways, power consumption, fresh financial architectures, world currency regulation, and unification of confessional systems etc – are rapidly becoming daily* macrotasks. Albeit ones which cannot be handled inside existent international structures and institutes. Ironically then, it is also necessary to react in a timely fashion towards speedy changes occurring in the here and now.

At this juncture, we must confront questions concerning a **global control system for civilization and any regulation of world processes** - which, towards the end of the XX, as well as the beginning of the XXI centuries, brought themselves to public attention. At first glance, the initial stages of global management will hopefully engender reasonable conversations on the creation of a world legislature (world parliament), an executive body (world government), judicial authority (world court), not to mention a security council and a world religious union. Thus, it is necessary to make use of all inherited experience regarding the development of humanity: including the UN, EU, G-8, G-20, along with other relevant international organizations, institutes and so on. Considering this is the most radical set of questions, there will be many opponents to such a discourse. So, lets begin this dialogue by brainstorming, i.e. carrying out various conferences and forums similar to Davos. Indeed, we contend formulations of any macropurpose serving humankind have reached a level whereby civilization can solve the global problems facing it. Certainly, from the moment humanity (theoretically) left Africa, we human beings have lived through approximately 100 thousand years: existing in a recognizable form for about 5000 generations. Indirectly implying, as this does,, we inhabitants of the XXI century are destined to recapitulate world history before transmuting our society into a type 1 planetary civilization in (allegedly) 100-150 years. A transition of momentous significance in the very nick of time.

CHAPTER II

Global challenges, times of variation and radical changes

Today's world is undergoing a tremendous change: economic crises, global warming, food shortages, famine and other calamities are compelling complex socio-political transition. Each change engulfing the whole planet and propelling cultural elites and national authorities to take managerial steps ahead of time. Steps trying to avoid a loss in credibility with the public, while searching for new solutions to every problem.

Indisputably, the mortgage crisis of 2008 presented us with an issue that speedily transformed into a general economic affliction affecting most of the developed economies. A calamity proving so profound it is (nowadays), compared to the Great Depression of the 1930s. Furthermore, unemployment rates have soared worldwide; a setback penetrating into social spheres wherein it produces a negative impact on living conditions - due to lower incomes and a significant increase in food prices. Triggering, one might add, massive social dilemmas in a number of prosperous nations. Especially, perhaps, within many thriving economies in the Middle East and North Africa, where these exact troubles have resulted in social revolutions overthrowing a number of national governments. Admittedly, experts in these fields predict a second wave of cultural hurdles, which will affect most countries worldwide. An event likely to force 'the world government' represented by the G8 and the G20 to initiate a revolutionary monetary reform to replace the crashed US dollar with a world's reserve currency in order to support and improve the regulatory mechanisms of financial markets. Thereby, establishing a fairer international trade environment and stabilize food prices [4, 5].

Atop this, natural environmental issues, **such as global warming** - which is known to cause floods, droughts, as well as the spread of epidemic diseases across our world - quite rightly initiates anxiety among the public. Now a proven fact, it is said that by the mid-twenty-first century the fossil-based economy will be a major contributor towards this phenomenon. At present, people can no longer deny the Earth is gradually heating. And as such, over the last hundred years, the mean temperature on our planet has clearly risen by 0.7 °C - a growth rate exponentially increasing. If this scenario persists, of course, scientists predict that before the centuries end, the total growth in temperature will have exceed 2 °C - which might entail catastrophic consequences.

Everything being analysed, persistent **social inequality and moral degradation**, along with widespread political corruption (coupled with the inefficiency of local authorities and their indifference to the needs of ordinary people), also need to be named as the twin factors plaguing many regions of our Earth. In themselves, they *represent some of the most significant catalysts in those areas for crime and violent atrocity.*

All things considered, large-scale corruption, with its diversity of forms and high levels of organization, is comparably destructive in developing economies. Representing, as it does, a big hurdle on the way to further development in the international community. Moreover, truly effective means to combat corruption are yet to be discovered.

Tangentially, new global challenges facing humanity will soon be identifiable by **analysing the underlying processes** presently occurring in the international economic arena: in geopolitics and in international relations. Indeed, a second wave of "measurable" global crises was foreseen as potentially causing another economic depression in 2013-2015. Taking into account, however, the cyclical nature of economic development, a third wave of noteworthy crisis is actually expected in 2017-2019. Thence, beginning in 2020, after all the essential innovations for the sixth technological cycle have emerged, the global economy will go into a long upturn. Experts predicting that rapid economic growth leveraged by new technologies of the sixth techno-cycle will thereafter begin in 2025 - provided humankind avoids getting into a global nuclear conflict [7]. Obviously, such conflicts might be ignited between nuclear powers in one of the currently existing conflict areas. What is more, countries with nuclear arsenals already include the USA, Russia, Britain, France, China, India, Pakistan, North Korea and Israel – a list which keeps growing. All meaning that the potential casualties of war between any of them may reach as high as 2.5 billion lives within a combat zone. Each fatality a result of military operations, nuclear attacks, or radiation sickness. Additionally, 1.5–2 billion people across our planet would have severe to medium radiation exposure from contaminated air, water and food. Therefore, considering the global conveyor of prevailing winds and water currents, only a few hundred million people will be lucky enough to find themselves in low-exposure regions. Uncontaminated water and clean food being a rare and highly valued resource. This may be our possible future.

Even nowadays, this speculated, millions of people worldwide suffer poverty, hunger and hardship. The industrialized countries of the world (we collectively refer to them as the G20 / G8) - despite existing plans for long-term national strategic development – are still unable to formulate any concrete solution to the protracted crisis persisting in the world's economy. Possibly because their agendas often revolve around the idea of earning excessive profits and securing their own leadership in the race for economic supremacy. Additionally, the excessive spread of the US dollar in recent years has resulted in the volume of available (global) money outgrowing the production of planetary goods by 10–12 times. The laws of economics, however, dictate that such a huge imbalance will inevitably cause a slump. Explaining why so many rich countries have been using recent advances in science and technology to maximize their fiscal growth in the name of continued prosperity. An untenable situation demanding that the global elites (including billionaires and powerful politicians (political clans)) change their attitude and turn toward our international community of nations governed by the UN and other cross-cultural organizations.

In these challenging circumstances, the UN, the International Monetary Fund, the European Bank for Reconstruction and Development, the

International Bank for Reconstruction and Development, along with the European Union - as well as other international financial and public institutions, have failed to achieve maximum efficiency in their undertakings. Simultaneously, industrial advancement in the III-IV-V-techno-cycles has come to a standstill. In which case, our civilization must enter the new VI technological cycle in order to carry on planetary economic progress through the decades to come (2020-2050).

Everything taken together, thinking about the formation of a **new global control system** defending humanity against worldwide crises, accidents, climate change and other negative processes (or for that matter blatant military threats), must remain at the top of human civilizations schedule. Hence, the following section is devoted to those searches for novel ways within which to proceed as a species on the move.

CHAPTER III

Conceptual models of transition to a post-industrial civilization (A systematic approach)

A world crisis looms. The reasons for it are systematic ones. Even the best minds on our planet are researching ways to escape from the current situation. The difficulty, however, is that certain portions of humankind live like parasites, while earthquakes, atmospheric warmth, water security and starvation plague our modern era. So, billions face deficiencies in basic resources, yet our sphere is additionally shaken by social, economic and political instability. To our thinking, the latter phenomena being exacerbated by ignoring objective economic laws, as well as clear cultural principles (8,9).

Hence, the world is near an abyss. Its further development is in danger... all signalling that a change of consciousness is necessary. A radical adaptation within world psychology, reviving spirituality, moral values and a general sense of responsibility. As such, it is time for humankind to settle the affiars of its own house. A challenge initially thrown down to developed countries (G8, G20), but one eventually extending to the entire world community. This is where the sciences come into their own. Especially the type of objective assessments leading to the preservation and evolution of life, along with sustainable planetary progress. In this regard, a quote from the UN's General Secretary Ban Ki-moon to "Rio +20" in 2012 may be pertinent: "The planet is in a condition of unprecedented crisis. We need to recognize that the present model of global development is irrational. We risk bringing doom to a billion people through poor conditions of endemic poverty. It is necessary to find a new way to advance forward ...".

It is the job, this acknowledged, of scientists to create innovations and technical openings. But, even Nobel Prize laureates aren't privileged to see how these modernizations will affect the various spheres of political existence. So, despite distinctions in prevailing opinions, this crisis (as was already mentioned is system one [6,10]) rapidly approaches. Any solution, therefore, should be investigated via systems integrity and adequacy to the task. Deliberately humanistic outlooks providing the key to safety as a basis for world order.

*Obviously, then, it is necessary to change prevailing views on market economies. In our opinion, **post-industrial civilization only dawns after a radical economic revisioning**. A vision inclusive of new knowledge, science and high technologies, an equilibrium between capital and all ranges of spiritual upgrading, along with an updating of value systems.*

When considering problems on this general plane, it is possible to notice the following. Benefit would immediatey be derived from global schools of sciences, wherein thinkers stood up for control over population growth: others for the observance of doctrines (strategies towards eternal life), and - last but not least - a conscious building of the noosphere. Yet, our world moves in unpredictable ways. Meaning, of course, scientific solutions to fundamental dilemmas only comes nearer once a problem is completely clarified. Worded differently, a systematic elimination of world crises, global threats and so on, is possible through consistant development alone.

Objectively speaking, contemporary Capitalism and Socialism are on the threshold of Renaissance-level changes. Truely, the time of post-industrial civilization has come. Space exploration too. A noosphere era. An entry into other systems of coordinates and values beyond present day comprehension. Thus, our claim that **the third wave of human development is here**. Born, as it is, from the fractures betwixt Capitalism and Socialism, it is (in real terms) a direct **transition to innovative economic practice in post-industrial civilization (innovatsionizm)**. Unarguably, our XXI century, with this perspective before us, is best seen as the century of the noosphere. In itself, a break with previous conditions, because any "noosphere-civilization" embraces cultural activities on Earth and in space. Creating, thereby, technological breakthroughs. For this reason, we are attemting to undertake a process of integration among separate scientific and technical, ecological, economic, atmospheric, spiritual and humanistic disciplines. Such a systems approach, using recent discoveries in every field, constructs revolutionary solutions to problems at a macrolevel deserving public attention.

On the basis mentioned above, we as authors make the bold assertion that attempts to step beyond post-industrial civilization necessitate all six Basic Elements of transition, i.e., the spiritual, new scientific and technological advances, a greening of society and the environment, space exploration, world safety and economy stability. Each of these factors demanding systemic consideration as a totality.

When all is done and dusted, the scientific novelty of this megaproject consists in a complex consideration of all aforementioned elements (i.e. basic components) as a uniform world outlook. A stance from which planetary control systems - and a regulation of global processes permitting the possibility of sustainable preservation - arise as active transitional states towards post-industrial civilization (figure 4).

To be fair, it is vital we notice that openings have already been made: even though they couldn't provide continuous development due to their unsystematic character. Overall, some research routes succeeded, while others lagged behind. For example, developments in G-8 and G-20 countries - where excess profits for multinational companies form the major incentive behind production - saw progress occur without a spiritual component. A sad fact even recognized by billionaires (B. Gates and others). Nonetheless, we authors grasped the consequences of this limitation in terms of a new stage of civilization.

Furthermore, as new methodologies connect current achievements in natural sciences (STP) with public perceptions, humanization (along with the essential resource of religions) is paramount in the suggested design of a planetary house. Thusly, we will briefly comment on each of the six blocks (figure 2).

BLOCK 1. HUMANIZATION WITHIN OUR GLOBAL COMMUNITY AND THE LOGICAL DEVELOPMENT OF WORLD HISTORY.

Global upheavals lead to adverse social and political changes[11]. These changes are like tremors, - occurring first in one place, then in others. Yet, changes can't be predicted accurately, since some can arise worldwide. What is more, a planetary crisis forces those in power to take preventative measures in order to avoid mistrust between people, or delay much needed recovery.

Essential factors in world communal development have, therefore, been studied for many years - despite social repression, spiritual degradation, political corruption, idleness by local authorities and their indifference to the needs of people in various regions of the world [7]. Many countries, stated so, even lack an active national ideology: having lost their sense of social orientation. A diminution eventually followed by thoughtless consumption. Thus, the ethnic idea (focussing on the consciousness of a people), is necessary for most political mechanisms. Being based, as it tends to be, on the perceptions of a nation's unity, as well as an adaptation of its language, culture and customs. But the national idea is a not only a spiritual phenomenon. It is also integrally connected with ethnic interests and their realization. Hence, every nation that isn't capable of existing independently from other nations competes in a half-hearted manner with them.

Thenceforth, understanding a national idea, national interests and mutual trust, is an indispensable condition of progress [2].

In themselves, **World religions** poorly protect the population from moral decomposition and crime. Instead, they seem to foster these dysfunctions - seemingly incapable of generating spiritual revival, or national unification. All influencing international security across the world. Taken as a whole, of course, religion always plays a part in attempts to support its adherents by all means required. Yet, who will deny that religiosity doesn't make its believers happy?

It is conceivable, nevertheless, that the spiritual representatives of each faith could promote an **awakening of consciousness**. If so, their

congregants would find a full release from stereotypes: afterwards rec-
ommending the application of technologies to improve their physical
bodies – living temples without which consciousness can't realize itself
completely. Unfortunately, such representatives in the so-called developed
countries understand the opposite. For them, society's evolution throughout the centuries depended on market relations and private capital rather
than reason, or faith. In the face of deadly threats, however, it is time to
trust our spirits.

In this unstable century of globalization, that asserted, the idea of
humanization in society can become a factor of unification between
people's and states. After all, the implementation of mindful actions and
the use of centuries-old historical values will provide opportunities for an
unprecedented spiritual and cultural recovery. A huge step upholding honour in society, without which communities become stagnant. **The main
task of humanization being to change the thinking of a person
- his consciousness according to the requirements of a new civilized society in our XXI century.**

Now, any restoration of harmonious relations betwixt society and nature
in the XXI century is possible through the elimination of ethical shortcom-
ings – rather than the production and development of admittedly finite raw
material. Indubitably, a new vision, new ideas and new projects need implementation. Projects **following the laws of historical development**
accompanied by a practical spirituality.

So, in answer to questions like what will the new form of society be, it is
expedient to consider two factors.

**Firstly, how it uses the experience of worldwide historical
development from ages past** and, equally, its primordial national history - along with the spiritual-cultural values of each country, or region.

Secondly, how new requirements in the XXI century facilitate a **transition to a post-industrial humanistic noosphere-civilization.**
During its first stage, any developmental act requires investment capital to
innovative technology, to research and hone skills, not to mention assisting
human capital.

All the above additionally testifies that throughout world development there comes a moment of truth, when there will be a need to elaborate new global strategies for greater order. As such, it seems necessary to begin with the development of an outward looking political state ideology centered on the preservation of moral, spiritual-cultural values and traditions.

In which case. the key components of society's humanization are as follows (see Fig.1):

- *history of past, present and future;*
- *change of world psychology;*
- *revival of spiritual and moral values, along with world religions: including Islam, Christianity, Buddhism, Confucianism, etc.;*
- *harmonious development of society;*
- *creative development of human capital as well as a sharp decrease in world population;*
- *spiritual revolution in the XXI century.*

Ironically, the global crisis made us open our eyes. Reminding us, as it did, there are many reasons to try and **revive high moral and spiritual** values: internal treasures gathered by humankind over the centuries which today seem readily rejected by so many. Be that as it may, the world, once again, seeks the ideals of humanism and justice. Certainly, on today's Earth, one is witnessing public unrest, natural calamities and dictatorships arise for apparently no reason. All contributing to moral decline and the rupture of social ties resulting in a moral crisis.

Evidentially, **we forget about social humanization** at our peril. And once forgotten, the need to coexist under the same natural laws disappears from sight. These laws, however, only allow people to flourish if they meet ethical standards. An inbuilt principle demanding that Society always remembers the natural basis of development – Nature itself. Debated so, natural and human capital seem to decrease when the paramount significance of inherited cultural wealth is forgotten. It could be stated, therefore that if the laws of harmonious social development are broken, "the market's invisible hand" plays a role, whereby **rich states became hostages to the world crisis**.

In answering how global problems are to be resolved, we authors feel that the time has come to place before the UN **Concepts for a new spiritual and ideological doctrine of universal development**. A proposal lifting the spiritual resources of nations and nationalities into a working agenda. Finally, we contend there will be a transition to a post-industrial paradigm of spiritual development if this schemata is put into action (see fig. 2).

As a brief example, we will elucidate our view behind the much needed spiritual revival – beginning, as we must, in one of the Euroasian regions. Indeed, we will discuss **the creation of the NEW SPIRITUAL and TECH-NOLOGICAL CLUSTER "Turkestan Valley"** *(it is represented as a depiction of the West and East uniting via the Great Silk Way as a regional model: a new spiritual and technological development symbolizing international security) as a point of departure*. From history, it is known that ancient Turkestan was a spiritual center. All boding well for the restoration of this special place.

The main **objective** - which doesn't even have analogs in our international national megaproject – is to to turn Turkestan into the international spiritual center (megalopolis), as the first practical step in ensuring worldwide security. This would mark the actualization of our ideal in one region: thereby coordinating two especially large cardinal issues. To begin with, the spiritual and cultural unification of society and, secondly, a new, sixth technological way. Presented, as it must be, to the entire globe as a new Renaissance of multidimensional opportunities [12]. Around Turkestan, after all, a number of countries are settled (approximately 400 million people may be inhabitants in our ideal) to capacity.

The difference, of course, between this project and, say, **Silicon Valley** in the USA would be the harmonious blending both spiritual and cultural collaboration. A bold assertion of innovative sixth technological methods encouraging mutual human benefit.

At the international level, "New Turkestan" will unite West and East once again. Attracting, as it is bound to, opportunities all the way along the

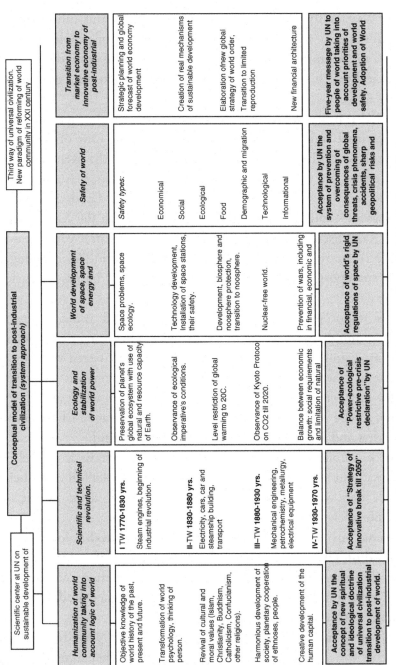

Figure 2: Construction of a survival strategy of mankind in XXI and futher centuries

Great Silk Way. With a centuries-old history behind it, this culture project will then doubtlessly adapt the spiritual consciousness of people generally. Indeed, as a move promoting unity amid people who are grounded in environmental realities, it will additionally encourage higher-order goals across this region.

In the XXI century, we suspect new morals will also be created, which previous spiritual and cultural institutes must explore. One of these centres of speculation being located within Turkestan. Yet, the overall purpose is not to create state territories for the sake of it. Rather, it is an attempt to construct areas of transformation for humankind. Lands integrating all of Euroasian - and ensuring international security in the XXI century. Moreover, Kazakhstan needs to declare itself as a nuclear-free country, even though it has the richest uranium deposits in the world. All meaning, a "Baikonur spaceport" could be built from appropriately harnessed nuclear energy one day.

The most important thing, all of the above recognised, is that as a result of managing uniform process coordinating spiritual-cultural development, new innovative and technological methods will be discovered whereby an effective use of that most expensive capital – human beings – is discovered. Such know-how, of course, gives encouragement to the whole world. **Put differently, in the XXI century, this project will courageously step into new thoughts and higher-consciousness for humankind.**

Within this project, so understood, the center of Eurasia is unlikely to reanimate without a new Turkestani spiritual and technological valley being formed, i.e. there will be a new megalopolis undergoing development as a clear example of evolutionary activities (Fig. 3).

At present, our world lacks clearly spiritual and technological projects focused on civilized development. It is almost as if anxiety and fear prevented this kind of revolution in consciousness. **Hence, our enthusiasm in offering a megaproject complete with exemplary models of new spiritual and technological benefits.**

In itself, New Turkestan will turn Euroasian into a place for cultural wealth across the region. All resulting in social unity wherein people work in unison towards sustainable development. Thus, as soon as this regional project yields results, its universal symbolism will create a naturally progressive agenda. Obviously, Turkestan as a spiritual capital should be administered under the auspices of the UN - with assistance from UNESCO. Its representative offices and officers being adept inside international organizations and institutes. Needless to say, this example of post-industrial civilization always puts the human factor at the forefront of its thinking. True science, culture, education, health, religion, moral and other universal values, becoming the flags under which it flies.

Globalization must begin in the spiritual sphere. Only then, will this project lead to law, consent, and peace within international relations. Sharp reorganizations, therefore, of spiritual consciousness, along with radical changes in world psychology are necessary. Each transition starting with a fundamental reconsideration of former ideological postulates. For instance, from an economic point of view, production needs to focus on the consumption patterns of a **specific person**. Without this base, so-called "excessive" consumption gives misleading data. Information testifying that the requirements of today's humanity would need a planet 1.5 times bigger than our Earth (by ecological organization Global Footprint Network.). Either way, to reduce humanities negative influence on nature, every individual has to eat less meat, make sensible choices between cars and bicycles and live simply in order that other may simply live.

BLOCK 2. SCIENTIFIC AND TECHNOLOGICAL REVOLUTIONS

Humanity is on the march. We are taking our first steps into a new, post-industrial socially oriented civilization, whose main driver is the progress in science and technology. Most of the developed nations of our world (guided in their endeavors by the Theory of Long-Waves), are now completing the fifth technological cycle ..... and are actively engaged in building the foundation for the sixth techno-cycle. Core factors include the following -

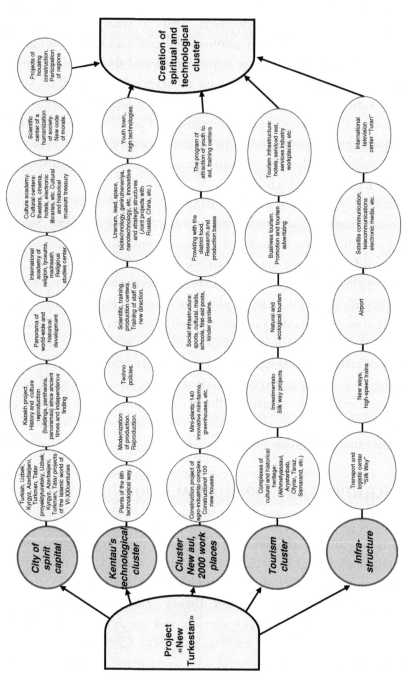

Drawing3 Network model of international megaproject "New Turkestan"

Yet, the next technological cycle will see the rise of biotechnologies, nano-technologies, genetic engineering, information and communication networks, artificial intelligence and space technologies. **Extreme innovation appearing to be an appropriate solution to the global crisis. A panacea, which means developing strategies for unrestrained breakthroughs through large-scale international development programmes tailored for specific clusters.**

To maximise the conditions required for a transition of this sort, it is advisable to modernise education and public health. An undertaking, which will quicken the advent of the new techno-cycle. A strategy outlined in the above core areas, even though each necessitates a comprehensive cluster-programme when applying all of the enhanced knowledge into practical usages.

Later on, after the VI techno-cycle has been fully expressed (possibly by 2050), our global economy will enter the next long-wave technological cycle at a new level of post-industrial civilization.

Yet, before full results in the VI technological revolution are achieved, a period of deep geopolitical and geoeconomic transformations may be foreseen. Essential changes, no doubt, influencing the entire demographics of our planetary population. Certainly, considering everything together (with G8, G20 participation), it is desirable for structural divisions in the UN to acquire an in-depth knowledge of our worlds historical development. Also, it would prove helpful for them to study insights into human origins, so that the strongest possible base for scientific and technical information-facilitates are constructed. Equally, structural divisions inside the UN (together with the states G8, G2) may, thereby, **predict international problems in the XXI century through roleplayed scenarios anticipating both decisions and measures.**

The future belongs, therefore, to a "knowledge-bank" of intellectual economics. All presenting a creative opportunity for society: accompanied by an accumulation of value-systems building a post-industrial civilization. In this way, a superior position is taken by countries with higher scholarly resources, because new information technologies (Internet resources) invite investment. Although they cannot resolve safety issues within our proposed planetary house.

Globalization, in itself, has shown researchers that any transition from a market economy into an innovative post-industrial economy is fraught with complications. However, our projected approach is completely new. Representing, as it does, a fresh paradigm for world governance. Albeit the type of theoretical model requiring rational interaction. Once grasped, productive processes must take into account spiritual and historical elements as vital components of the theorem. Indeed, during the final formation of technology-wave VI, the very balance of our world necessitates it.

In a manner similar to the classic Liberal thinkers, we authors postulate that increasing competitiveness can be beneficial. Beyond question, post-industrial civilization will put it at the forefront of positive human factors. Furthermore, science, culture, education, health, religion, morality and other (universal civilization) values will openly observe socio-economic progress through this freedom. Far-sighted authorities even nowadays praising such liberty as progressive.

Additional investments generated in this way will increase expenditure on healthcare, science and education. Thereby giving a new impulse to the development of innovative technological methodologies. In this regard, the first quarter of the XXI century will create new institutes, revive moral systems and evolve advanced ethical values. This is why international organizations and public forces have to favour these changes. Otherwise, unruly social fragmentation will fall into fierce social conflicts - as occured in a number of Eastern countries. Hence, some have claimed these policies alone can preserve peace.

Tellingly, globalization will appear most strongly in the spiritual sphere. This will inevitably lead to progressive statements in law, since **consent** and peace will guide international relations. A transition also encouraging a reconsideration of former ideological postulates on a number of mundane levels.

Living progressively, for example, even though it is known that there are more than 1.2 billion people starving at the moment, will foster new hope among the nations. In this regard, it is **expedient to make sure there are minimum barriers to normal life** in order to increase competitiveness within the economy of human capital (**see fig. 1**). In addition, it will advance the following:

- ***health care*** *(health care financing according to the recommendation of the World Health Organization must be be no less than 6% of GDP);*
- ***science*** *(financing within the sciences has to be no less than 1.5% GDP);*
- ***education*** *(no less than 6% GDP);*
- ***culture*** *(no less than 5% GDP);*
- *formation of intellectual economies for the creation of artificial intelligence;*
- *realization of individual consumption balanced against a competitive standard of living.*

Only by establishing **minimum social and economic standards** (of life) in the field of human capital, is it possible to provide a really comfortable existence. Thence, having coordinated minimum standards for growth rates within the economy it will be possible to define norms and qualities of life for developing Third World countries. Clearly, these norms would provide high rates of economic growth depending on the abilities of each person and the concomitant competitiveness of their nation.

At such, people will know in advance that without an increase of competitiveness in human capital, it is impossible to reach a high standard of living. Everyone, however, aspires to it. Without it, people won't be persuaded to embrace advanced ideologies, or religious trends.

All resulting in a fair approach to everyone on this planet (due to identical conditions), wherein peace and harmony will prosper. Moreover, increased, but healthy, competitiveness between countries will be created. In our opinions, this is induced by various methods: including those which meld both capitalist, and socialist modes of production. Following this, rising living standards will gradually align citizens lives across our world.

Only the question of present day moral degradation remains a threat. One of the main signs of it is **professional incompetence** in all spheres of human capital: from the lowest level to the highest ones, including public administration.

Obviously, this is more visible in developing countries. Nevertheless, even developed countries (during their recent crises) experienced acute failings in risk-management. Thusly, the EU urgently allocated funds to train unqualified personnel in order to stabalise growth rates for unemployment across Europe.

Coincidentally, it is at these junctures that **new paradigms about an educated society** are born. Amid conditions of global crisis, science and education often come to the forefront of events and form the **basis of advanced systems for production cycles.** Each being a pattern for qualitative education, science, spirituality and revived cultural values. If one wants to preserve peace, then education must be understood as a public benefit - instead of a social burden. An idea prophesying a XXI century formation of "intellectual capital" as a foundation of real progress. A notion especially effective when receiving new knowledge through which University graduates can secure work, rather than being unemployed.

Eventually, every social spheres has to work towards spiritual production as an ultimate. Human capital is then a significant part of this multilayered equation. Thus, key factors developing this essential human component are **investments into people themselves and an establishment of genuine cultural freedom promoting real choice.** The UN as an organization could exercise supervision of these indicators by regulating and coordinating various bodies providing sustainable enlargement. A scheme monitored by the UN itself through the creation of a **World advisory council.** Established so, a **5-yearly Message to people of the world** could become a regular update on progressive ideals and their implementation. Every announcement designed to be as inclusive as possible during that stage of the overall megaproject.

BLOCK 3. ECOLOGY AND STABILIZATION OF PLANETARY ENERGY CONSUMPTION

According to scientists, humankind is now approaching the first phase of global ecological disaster. But a "point-of-no-return" haven't, as yet, been reached.

This is probably due to the fact our biosphere has huge resources which (although used by humankind) defy complete exhaustion. However, even conservative commentators are starting to become clearly concerned: waring us about potentially cataclysmic events towards the turn of the current century. In this regard, the preservation of our planetary global ecosystem by newly devised and rational technologies is vital. Unsurprisingly, this noted, present measures by some experts grimly warn us all that if humanity doesn't take urgent measures to preserve our ecosystems, then ecological death may result as soon as the XXI century. In other words, the first phase – a phase of global ecological decline [9] has started. A respected scientist in the field, N. Moiseyev, even claiming there is a possibility of stability loss for the entire biosphere as a complete system [13].

In our opinion, local problems were being solved one by one. Yet, attempts by the USA and the former USSR to draw underdeveloped regions into their respective spheres of influence have more or less thwarted this process. Indeed, trying, as these superstates were, to create a balance of forces between them, the USA and USSR proved more concerned with providing political stability than ecological sustainability. However, after the collapse of the USSR, any responsibility for guiding humankind into futurity fell to the USA. Sadly, this acknowledged, it appears to be in no hurry to shoulder this burden.

Currently, therefore, our problems are on a planetary scale. All meaning, our Earths biosphere and noosphere need international collaboration, as well as ecological, maintenance. Irrespective, then, of a states' status, it is necessary to find compromise solutions. Answers to otherwise intractable issues teasing out fruitful destinies for human civilization.

Despite the rapid growth of NTP, power-elites will continue to dominate the means and modes of energy. An issue that will haunt development in future high technologies. Yet, the globe still needs enormous quantities of fuel. With this in mind, the problem of stabilizing world power consumption must work towards 10 bln.n.e. generation – making our theoretical "house" into a mansion. [14]. Finding a balance, after all, between effective power consumption and growth in our Earths population (while maximizing social opportunities) becomes a question of visionary planning. Each projected scheme demanding standards of **per capita power consumption,** along with a decreased, or restrictive, use of fossil fuels. Certainly, it may be necessary to apply a differentiated scale, wherein a classification of consumption is developed through the various levels of energy consumption. Unquestionably, all these issues have to be widely discussed by energy-experts: UN working groups taking the lead through specific UN sessions.

As for observance of the Kyoto Protocol on CO2, signatories are bound till 2020. However, it is a toothless tiger unless the USA, the People's Republic of China, the entire EU, India and Russia implement these agreements. Time, this asserted, is not on humanities side - and unless radical measures to reduce greenhouse gas emissions to safe levels are introduced - things look bleak. In this particular scheme, neither the Copenhagen conference (2009), nor the UN conference on sustainable development ("Rio +20"), really helped to solve this matter. Probably, initially, it is necessary to establish rigid sanctions and tax regulations on CO2 emissions. Secondly, it is essential that a **global power ecological fund** is created to further stimulate this process.

Obviously, special sessions at the UN, as well as meetings of the G-20 (with its connection to respected politicians, ecologists, climatologists), would play a fundamental role in changing official policies. Moreover, adopting a directional convention may solve two-uniform problems: on the one hand, a transition to **energy saving technologies** (an application of light-emitting diodes, electric cars etc) and on the other hand, a transition to **renewable energy sources** (wind, sunlight, hydrogen, thermonuclear energy, magnetism etc.). In which case, consumption of energy will exponentially decrease because of reusable resources. For example, solar energy technologies are scarce at the moment, about - 0,5%. Contrarily, its annual production grows at 45%, i.e. every two years it almost doubles.

There are plans to implement solar power stations across our globe. In this respect, the USA, the People's Republic of China and a number of other countries are working diligently.

Restricting, of course, global warming to 20C was confirmed as an aim by a UN declaration adopted in Copenhagen at the International Conference on Climate Change (2009). But, unfortunately, even the UN – the most authoritative organization in this field, can't interfere inside sovereign nations. In itself, testifying that it's status is insufficient to solve global problems. Additionally, there is no political will by governments, even though they claim to be concerned. So, when the ecological crisis comes, addressing these issues may be too late.

All making pundits conclude that new planetary conditions, global cataclysms, geophysical accidents, climate warming, food crises and the much needed transition to innovative technologies, demands a Central Asian focus. Its implementation requiring the creation of working groups of experts, analysts, independent scientific organizations and strong minds. Perhaps, then, it is time to create (under UN guidance) a new body – a **Supreme council of wise men from all over the world**.

Summing up, we note that if the humanization of culture is at all possible, we need a **harmonious development between society and nature** in the XXI century. A planetary house, in other words, of universal civilization **(see figure 1)**. The quintessence of all these actions recommended by the UN and advised as a restrictive pre-crisis declaration **(see figure 2)**. The era of fossil fuels is over. Instead, an economy-of-energy providing normal, comfortable, safe alternatives is at hand - excluding accidents and ecological crises.

To our minds, if environmental conditions become overly detrimental, the UN has every right to seize control over sources of power and their effective use for the benefit of all humankind. To prevent such moves in advance, it is necessary for a **change in existing models of economic growth** - especially in developed countries. For instance, a decrease in annual profits, while investing in high-energy saving technology, would either delay, or halt, the forthcoming crisis.

Avoiding this impasse of a "Death Valley" scenario by exploring the noosphere for inspiration, will engender spectacular results. It will encourage new paradigms of consumption based on emerging VI technological methods. Nonetheless, to achieve this revolutionary jump, huge efforts of partnership in world civilization are necessary.

BLOCK 4. DEVELOPING SPACE TECHNOLOGIES, ALTERNATIVE ENERGY SOURCES AND THE RESOURCES OF OUR SOLAR SYSTEM

Ever since the beginning of the space exploration era, military circles in every superpower have contemplated military applications for space technologies. Yet experts and humanitarians, like **Prof. Vladimir Vernadsky,** put moral values above material ones, whereas the reality of so-called 'technological man' in our present day seems to reverse this scale [15].

Humanity will always keep demanding more and more energy, of course, whether from cosmic nature or otherwise. A demand linked to the progress of our human race itself. Be that as it may, science and technology will not always be ready to provide power in ever-increasing proportions. Yet, as we know from history, we can expect new discoveries and inventions (such as the teleportation of atoms), which will enable humankind to make another technological leap forward in pursuit of better horizons. Notably, the fantastic predictions made many years ago by Leonardo da Vinci, Jules Verne, Benjamin Franklin, Nostradamus and the Marquis de Condorcet have now become an everyday reality. Indeed, in the nearest future, solar power and hydrogen power will dominate the energy balance, whilst their market share today is only 0.5% of total human consumption.

Accordingly, **V. Vernadsky** [15] wrote: "We endure no crisis exciting weak souls, but one marking a great change in Mankind's thought. This time is coming, truly, even though it only happens once during a millennium. Standing on this change, peering at a revealed future, we have to be happy that we are fated to endure it and to participate in the creation of such a future". A huge contribution to developing the noosphere-civilization was, so noted, made by the following scientists: **I. Kant, Zh. Lagrange, A. Einstein, V. Vernadsky, N. Moiseyev, K. Tsiolkovsky, P. Kuznetsov, R. Bartini, A. Chizhevsky.** In the XXI century, the noosphere will enhance a surge forward in universal civilization.

In post-industrial civilization, thenceforth, land-based sources of energy will be exhausted and proven insufficient: ultimately being discarded [3].

In these conditions, space technology, a use of zero-point energy and the resources of our Solar system itself, will be used to establish international stability [9].

Earth-based energy sources will, no doubt, become depleted anyway - and will not be sufficient to satisfy the needs of our post-industrial civilization [15]. Environmental concerns will equally put further restrictions on the use of such sources of power. Space exploration, with a view to harnessing cosmic energies and tapping into the resources of the solar system, will, therefore, play a vital role in maintaining order as well as structure on our world.

We don't know whether there are other civilizations in space, or on other planets. Thus, having found routes into space, humanity must uphold itself through intellectual, spiritual, moral and humanistic values adequate to meeting possible civilizations on other worlds. From this perspective, it is unreasonable to connect sustainable development with a continuous use of non-renewable natural resources. A wise use of renewables, allied to the resources of the noosphere, however, make it possible to approach a sustainable development for humankind.

Our time period - up to the final expression of the VI technological way - will be an era marked by deep geopolitical and geoeconomic transformation. Clearly, the world's population structure will undergo a significant change. Taking the above into consideration, it is advisable that the United Nations (together with the G8/G20) form a joint institution maintaining the most complete database of scientific and technical knowledge, which may be required to implement a megaproject of any nature: or satisfy a request for assistance in transferring new methodologies to less adept parts of our globe.

Any long-term formation of integrated socio-cultural systems aiding our transition to a humanistic-noosphere-civilization, will be the result of global "revolution". Hence, it is necessary to understand that settling on other planets in our Solar, or other systems, should become the main task of people on Earth! Literally, in the next few years (thanks to achievements in theoretical and applied physics) satellites designed for an analysis of gravitational radiation in space will uncover unearthly civilizations elsewhere.

Phrased differently, humankind will witness the beginning of a radical cosmic era. Already "Rosetta" probes have successfully flown around Comets in exploratory trial runs.

If humanity endures, we will see the turning point of history. Our Age, connected as it is with pre-existing forms of historical development (themselves characterised by the enrichment of the banking classes, multinational companies and egoistical individuals, etc), will be identified by future civilizations as barbaric. They will say, our social stratification was scarred by huge discrepancies between rich and poor: by the starvation of 1.3 billion people; by a shortage of water and other basic needs.

Thankfully, a fast development of VI-TW will occur. A veritable leap forwards, whereby humankind starts to manage its relationship with the noosphere. Hardly recognised at present, the noosphere is still far beyond reasonable control: unlike our biosphere. Its utilization, that stressed, would have allowed (for example), an earlier correction of errors during the recent "mortgage meltdown" in the USA. An economic problem draining considerable funds and causing disruption far outside of its boundaries.

The development of humanity in the XXI century, on a basis of increased economic efficiency and competitiveness, has to arrive at the following stage – i.e. once **a joint solution of global problems through interstate, intercontinental and interplanetary balance** is achieved. At this stage alone, will humankind shoulder its planetary tasks. Certainly, an association of efforts by all people in our world on a basis of mutual respect, the principles of social justice, and a refusal to participate in wars, or violence, will establish general harmony.

Unlike previous problems occurring before the XXI century, when hundreds of millions of lives were lost as a result of wars, accidents, and other cataclysms, from now onwards, these ills will be addressed from the perspective of an integrated noosphere-civilization centred on absolutely new principles.

Hereafter, humankind should resolve a number of issues on a planetary scale and accept structural advances through international organizations – UN, IAEA, etc. Moreover, humankind should both create and introduce space technologies: install space stations and develop interstellar security.

Only then, will our biosphere and noosphere be fully protected. Obviously, this entails a transition to towards a nuclear-free world, the prevention of global wars (usually provoked by financial, economic, or unfortunate circumstance), intercontinental balance, regulations for the commercialization of space, power consumption regulations, and the advancement of solar energy. All unfolding under the close attention of our world community.

Approximately, during the thirties of the XXI century, when programmes for the commercialization of space will be addressed, obtaining energy from space will be possible: making it expedient for leading countries accross our world to collaborate. As there will be pilotless supersonic aircraft/rockets stationed in space, it will prove impossible to allow its militarization. Accordingly, J. Friedman forecast: "by the 50th year of XXI century, installations for receiving solar energy will already be in an orbit. In these years, one kilometer of geostationary Earth orbiting (streaming with solar energy), will be almost equal in energy-quantity to the energy containing in all the known oil fields of Earth" [23].

In our opinion, transition to a noosphere-civilization will induce humankind to renounce former stereotypes and will cure it of egoism and self-interest, thereby returning it to spiritual as well as moral values.

This "noosphere paradigm" imposes absolutely new requirements on humankind. First of all, it demands a much higher quality of general education. A position from which every person is faced with advanced in their moral frameworks: a structure wherein survival, stability and preservation govern affaires. Secondly, a transition from fiscal gratification, or mere enrichment –based on self-interested and short-term gains looks ridiculous. Certainly, these new types of knowledge will make such pursuits as obsolete as the dinosaurs. Instead, spiritual prosperity and peace on Earth will reign: allowing a much needed unification of humanity.

BLOCK 5. WORLD SECURITY

Our world nowadays, perhaps more than ever before, requires international collaboration in space exploration to ensure both world and regional security

[4]. As such, global scientific progress, whereby rates of knowledge multiply without censure, must be encouraged. Accordingly, American experts claim that the safety of the USA, let alone our world as a whole, will be under inevitable threat. Ironically, that said, the USA itself acts imperialistically through military escalation. Indeed, the direct military costs of this country went from % of the gross domestic product in 2001-2011 to 64% in more recent times. Furthermore, cumulative military expenses in the USA grew from 1 to 1.5 trillion dollars (or nearly 50%) compared to every other country taken together [22]. Sadly, the "arms race" between the USA, Russia, the People's Republic of China et al, will (potentially) lead to a number of "third world" wars during the 2020-2030 period. If this course isn't changed, expects predict continuing mayhem. Contrarily, these huge amounts of money could be spent on **joint projects** for space exploration, ecological improvement, security measures and the fight against climate warming etc. All necessary developments if we are to rescue our planetary house (**see figure 1**). It is vital, therefore, that we evolve mechanisms of mutual trust and transparency - otherwise any ban on the application of advanced weaponry (before general disarmament commences) must fail. For example, if there were restrictions and regulations on uranium enrichment (particularly laser uranium enrichment), then "third generation" nuclear bombs would hardly ever fall into the hands of terrorist organizations. Rather, a planetary economy arising from an **economy of new knowledge** would benefit humankind, as well as the emergence of futuristic superstates.

Yet, amid possible environmental terrorist attacks, climatic change and unforeseen cultural upheavals, it is possible to assume the next 20 years will witness an unnecessary cost in human life – some estimating millions of people will die [16]. Admittedly, not all experts share this belief, but such fears are understandable.

If these global crises manifest, of course, all of humankind will be irrevocably lost: neither high fences owned by billionaires, nor the police, or the army, will be in a position to save anybody. For that matter, neither will milliard investments on arms by the USA, Russia and China. Only a revaluation of our values will be sufficient to this task of genuine revival.

In this regard, the security issue must be seen as a single complete system, within which economics, society, ecology, food, demographics, scientific and technological information, power, space, and other types of safety, are framed (see fig. 2)

These types of safety require investigation and approval [15, 17]. In which case, experts from the UN should create basic principles of security, wherein the maximum permissible indicators characterizing every type of national safety are taken into rational account. Hence, we will consider further specified indicators as examples of practices engendering economic, social, demographic and ecological security.

Economic safety – at public institutes, which provide a guaranteed protection of national economic interests, not to mention effective socially directed structures, whereby a whole country generates sufficient economic resources in even the most adverse conditions.

Principles of ensuring economic safety for the state:

- *focus, an interaction of subjects regarding economic safety, a scientific justification for a continuity of actions – in time and in space, legality.*

Problems of ensuring national economic security:

- *timely forecasting and identification of external and internal threats to economic safety;*
- *ensuring equal and mutually beneficial cooperation between a specific state and other states of the world;*
- *increasing levels of competitiveness amid domestic industrial outputs on the basis of investment and innovative activity;*
- *increasing a population's level and life-quality of a country;*
- *maintenance of branches based of expanded reproduction for full population employment;*
- *creating a steady financial system which is equitable to interests, etc.*

Indicators characterizing a production sphere and its critical values are as follows:

share in industrial production, % - manufacturing industry; - mechanical engineering	70 25
the volume of investment into fixed capital, % to GDP	25
depreciation of fixed assets, %	40
share in export of manufacturing industry, %	40
labour productivity (thousands of dollars on one worker in prices and at par purchasing power), % - to the average world - to the developed countries	27,9 142 50

Financial safety - is usually characterized by stability in the financial systems of a country, whereas the stability of a national currency is maintained by a real exchange rate – providing the competitiveness of a national economy. Moreover, sufficiency in the volume of gold, along with foreign exchange reserves, maintain an active balance of payments, whereby favorable conditions are created for steady (high rate) economic growth.

Indicators characterizing financial safety and their threshold values are as follows:

rate of inflation, %	15
the volume of an external debt, % to GDP	25
share of external loans in covering budget deficits, %	30
budget deficit, % of GDP	5
the volume of foreign currency in cash – to the volume of cash in a national currency, %	25
monetary weight, % to GDP	50
gold and exchange stocks of a country, % to GDP	not less than 20
internal public debt, % to GDP	no more than 75
Balance of payments deficit, %	no more than 50

Basic principles for ensuring financial safety:

- ensuring the stability of economic development in a state;
- neutralization of impacts by world financial crises;
- ensuring stability in payment and settlement systems;
- prevention of a large-scale leakage of capitals abroad;
- prevention of crimes and administrative offenses in the financial sphere;
- attraction and use of foreign loans at an optimum for national economic conditions;
- stimulation by means of taxes to develop important activities for a country (economic activity, branches, regions, etc.).

Social safety is characterized by the security conditions of a population. Each of which is provided by a lack of high unemployment rates, degraded personalities, social conflicts, low levels of social tension, improved educational standards, health care, culture, science, qualitative foods and better living conditions.

Indicators characterizing social safety. Their critical values are as follows:

gap between the income of 10% (most prosperous population groups and 10% of the neediest)	8
Jeanie's coefficient (degree of deviation of actual distribution in monetary incomes and their equal distribution between inhabitants of the country)	0,3
population share with income lower than the a living wage, %	7
share living on less than 2.5 dollars a day	0,5
share of homeless and other socially declassed groups at % to the total number of the population	1,5
unemployment rates by Labour ministry, %	5
human development index, points	0,800
crime rate (quantity of crimes in 100 thousand people)	1000
alcohol consumption level per person in a year, litres	8
number of suicides in 100 thousand people	20
Prevalent levels of mental pathology in 100 people	360
share of the people consuming drugs, %	3,5

Basic principles of ensuring social safety:

- carrying out independent and socially focused economic courses;
- ensuring reproduction of social activities towards protected objects (person, society, state);
- ensuring protection of moral principles, customs and religious life, intellectual and information security;
- providing in the territory of a country personal security, constitutional laws and freedoms;
- strengthening of a law and the preservation of socio-political stability in society;
- timely forecasting and identification of external and internal threats to the social safety of the country;
- fight against terrorism strengthening drug businesses and smuggling.

Demographic safety – the ability of social systems to steadily function on the basis of population reproduction, seen as a process of continuous renewal in both number and structure through alternating generations.

The indicators characterizing demographic safety and their critical values are as follows:

Birth rate coefficient on 1000 ppl.	22
death rate per 1000 people	12,5
coefficient of natural increase in 1000 ppl.	12.5
migratory gain of people	1,1
share of migrants, % to numerical structure of the population	3
average life expectancy from birth, years	75
conditional coefficient of depopulation	1
general coefficient of birth rates in a population (average number of children born), ‰	2.15
coefficient of population aging, %	7
demographic loading of an disabled population on the able-bodied, %	60

Main objectives of ensuring demographic safety:

- improvement of social and economic conditions in a population;
- stage-by-stage providing and improvement of a state minimum for social standards in the fields of compensation, provision of pensions, education, health care, culture, housing-and-municipal services, social support and social services;
- optimization of external and internal migratory streams in a population;
- counteraction of illegal migration;
- formation of high spiritual and moral standards in citizens within the fields of family relations and increased family prestige;
- ensuring reproductive rights of citizens and assistance in the formation of high reproductive requirements in a population.

Ecological safety – a set of measures for the protection of personalities, society, and the state, from possible, or real, threats, which grow out of our human influence on the environment, along with natural disasters and accidents.

Critical values for indicators of ecological safety:

total receipts from ecological payments, % to GNP	5
ecological losses to GDP	5
nature protection costs for ecology, % to GDP	5
volumes of emissions in an environment of polluting substances	-
the saved-up quantity of radioactive waste demanding deactivation, special processing and lengthy storage	-
the areas of degraded lands, %	20

Basic principles for ensuring ecological safety:

- safety priorities for the life and health of personalities and society as a whole: universal values before any other fields of activity;
- prediction of ecological dangers for economic production;

- state and public supervision of ensuring ecological safety.
- allowing procedures and other activities capable of defending populations or territories;
- obligation of state environmental, sanitary, and epidemiologic facilities, to examination all construction projects, reconstruction, and productions;
- state support for actions improving either the habitat or person;
- organization of state systems for environmental monitoring;
- ensuring full, reliable, and timely knowledge for citizens, establishments, and organizations, about threats to ecological safety;
- publicity for plans of implementation defending the ecological safety of a population and an environment;
- broad participation in international activities regarding ecological safety;
- observance of the Kyoto Protocol.

In this way, UN experts can show the basic principles, tasks, indicators, and threshold values of the ten safety spheres. Furthermore, the UN could recommend them to members.

Block 6. Transitioning from a market economy to post-industrial exchange systems

As was specified earlier, the prospects for world economic development are manifestly improved by an **innovative economy.** A move which can be considered the most important advance in the XXI century (**see 10,11**).

Hence, the Founder of these "innovation concepts", Y. Shumpeter [18], argues that fiscal competition represents the main mechanism of resource gathering and efficiency growth: two of the driving forces of society as a whole.

Allied to this, scholars note that classical theories of "comparative advantage" were introduced by D. Ricardo [19], while similar ideas - regarding the stages of development in an economy - were developed by M. Porter [20], J. Stiglitz [5] and other scientists in the field.

So, globalization and world "crisis speculation" were revelatory. Especially when testing received theories like Keynesian economics and Monetarism. Indeed, both of these views appear to be right, provided previous assumptions and "revolution waves" are relied on as explanatory. Yet, the pursuit of excessive profit led to multinational corporations controlling more than half of our planets gross domestic product. Practices proving forgetful that sharp stratifications still exist in our society.

Therefore, scientific research into "competitiveness" - undertaken by the WEF (World Economic Forum), the International Institute of Management and Development (IMD, World Competitiveness Yearbook, Lausanne, Switzerland) and Harvard University (in particular) is extremely telling.

Life, for example, is said to quickly change inside globalized conditions. Particularly according to models engineered by M. Porter – a scholar who feels "objective" factors no longer have the strong impact they once enjoyed. Evidences making some claim there are new economic laws currently influencing markets and transforming them. From this perspective, the keys to our world economy have been transferred to financial oligarchs, the American Federal Reserve System (belonging to 20 private banks in the USA), international multinational corporations, international financial organizations – including the IMF, WB, and Country groupings such as the "Big seven". Moreover, a "Big 20" of the largest organizations, inclusive of the UN, NATO and the European Council, have practically ignored global economic processes in their service of the dollar.

Each a factor puzzling experts when it comes to the way in which any impending crisis can equip our proposed house of universal civilization, etc. (see figure 1).

At core, market systems for managing change seem to be built on lies. But humankind seeks for consciously operated process in the economy: procedures that eliminate the subjective roots of an economy. Far better would be objective causes motivating the transition to new systems of economic activity: blossoming, as it were, into a civilized economy. Something necessary at this point in history, as well as being the basic principal generating economic processes and reproduction cycles in the future.

In this regard, our task is to bring at least a scanty contribution to advanced civilization. Thus, block VI is devoted to the pressing question of "competitiveness" in our world economy. Firstly, (without repeating former mistakes), it is vital to enforce strategic planetary development: where we are going, in what ways we should conduct ourselves etc. However, some scholars don't even appear to know what they don't know.

Nonetheless, for first time in history the United Nations (as early as the nineties) put forward the idea of sustainable development. Although, on the way to planned purposes, there are certain difficulties: quite apart from the negative impact of the world crisis in 2008.

Of course, the ability *to forecast future events in geopolitics, ecology as well as socio-economics, let alone* determine strategic priorities for the world's economic advancement - thereby ensuring **sustainable growth** - has become a prime concern since the crisis of 2008 [10]. Clearly, on a pathway towards sustainable economic growth, **long-term projections** are not just a possibility, but rather a necessity for setting objectives and determining their fulfilment-strategies. Unfortunately, thus far, **no reasonable strategy for developing the world's economy within the context of ongoing globalization** has been conceived. Planetary mechanisms of strategic planning remaining, in themselves, underdeveloped.

Today, in addition to futurological notions, more and more long-term science-based forecasts are being published – some from 30-50 years into the future [11]. For instance, *The World in 2050* (2006), a forecast by Price Waterhouse Coopers, and *Dreaming with BRICs: The Path to 2050* [Wilson, Purushothaman 2003] by Goldman Sachs - never forgetting forecasts made by the Club of Rome, etc - have set the scene. However, the most appropriate tools to model global developments are represented by qualitative methodology - structural models, in other words, equally describing socio-economic processes. What is more, mathematical macro-modelling may be exercised as a method whereby long-term computer projection can detail the dynamics of our world's socio-economic evolution [17].

Considered so, it is advisable that the United Nations place an international order for the implementation of a **Concept for Strategic Planning of the World's Global Socio-Economic Development** with large interdisciplinary research teams and corporate support (**Fig. 4**).

Too many researchers, admittedly, are devoted to the problems posed by our worlds financial crisis. Without going into detail, however, scientists and experts are of the opinion that it is necessary **to find a uniform regulator for world currencies** making it possible to plan a ratio between global production, consumption and a specific monetary system: a rubric covering both goods as well as services. Thusly, it would prove possible to observe the mechanisms of production and capital regulation, while new financial architectures are constructed.

Overall, we have made an attempt to establish a definition of **uniform universal measurements for world currencies in the form of "power", i.e. the relation of kilowatts to currencies – kW/currency**. As such, this allow us to be rid of speculative capital with no real power [21]. Briefly the essence of this classification is as follows:

Any modern calculation of a gross domestic product in dollars is incorrect from the coefficient point of view: especially if recalculated in a number of currencies. So, a unit of power (for example, a kilowatt) can "cost" different amounts in the various currencies. Nevertheless, a kilowatt in Africa, America, Europe, or in Asia remains a kilowatt. All meaning it can be used to establish the rate of exchange between currencies worldwide.

For our purposes, we will present diagrammatic columns in table 1 (for countries, populations, economic opportunities). Regarding Europe, we will express the gross domestic product column in their Eurozone currency, for the USA – dollars, for Russia – rubles, for Kazakhstan – the tenge – also, we will try to express the cost of 0.1 watts in a national currency. Additionally, for simplicity, we will integrally take Europe, the USA, China, Russia, Kazakhstan and Belarus as cases. Moreover, economic opportunities (considered as a gross domestic products) will be expressed in gigawatts.

We tried to make a calculation of the economic opportunities in some countries - and the "fullness" of the national currencies of these countries in watts. Economic opportunities, therefore, represent the sum of power working towards generalized efficiency. Similar calculations can be carried out about any country on our planet.

Calculated algorithms of equal (fair) exchange rates ("costs") in any national currency looks as follows:

1. We determine a country's power in watts (through electricity consumption, fuels and food).
2. We define per Sq.m Unit the "quantity of money in the economy". Also, we set the ruble, dollar, euro, tenge etc, in watts. For example, 10 watt =1 ruble/tenge.

Thus, the "sovereignty" of a country isn't limited to its obligations. For example, to release an X amount of money into the global economy instead of Y raises practical implications. However, trade operations between a country's coefficient and currency recalculation will be worked out with kilowatts. A return, some would say, to when currencies had real a real basis (gold). Yet, the gold standard no longer points to a physical commodity lifted into abstraction.

Table 1 Economic opportunities for some countries in 2013.

Country	Popula-tion, mln. ppl.	GDP, Bln.US$	GDP per capita, (US$/person)	Economic opportuni-ties, GWt	Price of watt power, US$	Dollar sup-port, watts
USA	320,14	16 768	52 377	1 209,7	13,86	0,72
EU	506,04	16 666	32 935	864,9	19,26	0,52
China	1 357	9 181	6 766	1637,7	5,61	1,78
Russia	143,4	2 097,0	14 623	390,7	5,36	1,86
Kazakhstan	17,24	231,9	13 448	28,9	8,01	1,25
Belorussia	9,46	71,7	7 574	15,4	4,65	2,15
Ukraine	44,85	176,3	3 931	52,4	3,36	0,3

Figure4 Network model of global control system and regulation by world processes.

We established monetary weight (Sq.m) as a ratio of cumulative opportunities in a manner reminiscent of a country's "gold number" - F (Fibonacci's number) = 1,618033989 .... Now, the "gold number" is a constant: an ideal involving objects, systems or processes. Hence, estimates will be coordinated with Che. Montesquieu's statement (1689-1755) that "financiers support the state as rope does a hanged man".

If states don't cease their stupidly by slavishly following "world prices" and won't pass to an intelligent regulation of costs for exported production, then economic failure will be inevitable. Liberal markets, so-called, showing insolvency and susceptibility to crises of a cyclical character. Eventually, this being the case, the World Bank and the IMF will impose rules on countries for economic management. International organizations that could easily assume responsibility for reforming current world financial systems even though they show a lack of will, or simply an ability to "manage" affaires. Each one of them protecting interests, or infringing upon the interests of others. So, we need to be engaged in this task closely.

Overall, we recommend creating a Uniform currency union across the world with the following key tasks:

1. The basic rules of existence for a currency union consist in not attaching a currency **to a single good**. As such, it is necessary that a currency contains both force and power. Besides, the currency of any country shouldn't be expected to resist the temptation of attempting to dominate the world economy: although this risks crises and wars. Furthermore, pre-existent currencies like the dollar, or euro, are doomed to failure in any attempt to overtake other currency systems.

2. New currencies can't be tied to **leading world currencies**, since there is an **issue** regarding any currency overwhelming other currencies in terms of fixed power. An additional problem being discovered when the US dollar is unjustly valued against other currencies – for instance, that of the European Union, Japan, etc.

3. In trade operations between countries, when the coefficient of recalculation of currencies has to be **connected with kilowatts**.

4. When **an equivalent power is achieved**, it is necessary to calculate the security of currencies against real assets. It is supposed that such an approach will allow a transition from free to equal trade – even though the latter is speculative.
5. We believe also that any control of monetary weight (Sq.m) could be exercised by authorized intergovernmental bodies on the basis of corresponding **international treaties**.
6. In the case of a crisis, it is necessary to create an **intercurrency reserve fund**.

In summary, we note that the UN has to control the "cost" of all currencies worldwide (**filled with power**), and not allow any formation of currencies which haven't been based on real assets. In this regard, the United Nations is necessary to create a "currency commission" that can carry out an examination of ratios between currencies and their respective powers.

INSTEAD OF A CONCLUSION

1. On the question of where we go, it is possible to answer that only joint efforts worldwide can preserve humankind. Indeed, the USA, Russia, the People's Republic of China and other countries, along with the parallel progress of multinational companies, groups like the G8 and G20 and international financial organizations such as the IMF, the World Bank, WTO etc, are stepping in this direction. As are combined regional alliances such as the EU, NATO, BRIC, SCO and so on. Yet, unions alone won't solve global challenges.

In this transitional stage, therefore, it is necessary to begin true globalization with a reformed UN and other international organizations. Of course, when considering original paradigms for world development, it is vital to transform everything in the shortest of times. Hence, the UN may need to move its headquarters to another continent. Either way, the formation of a **functioning council for sustainable development** will be required, along with the creation of a **supreme council of wise men from across the world**: an executive secretariat of planetary ideology. Its influence similar to every other international organization (the WTO, for instance, isn't lower than the IMF or the World Bank, etc.) dealing with **priority global problems** like the financial crisis, climate change, the threat of of nuclear war, food security, space exploration and so on. This circle of tasks being set by the UN, the G8 and the G20. Although, the council of wise men must guide and oversee the UN, G8 and G20 etc.

All moves demanding the creation of a **world reserve fund,** financing joint global projects. Its tasks including .....

1. Formation of new structures for global control systems across the world. Also, the development of a medium-term / long-term roadmap to global sustainability.
2. Development of global warning systems that predict and mitigate threats, crises, technogenic disasters and natural calamities: severe geopolitical risks and conflicts of a social, political, astronomical, nature, etc.).
3. Development of criteria - and indicators - for an international system monitoring the progress of sustainable advancement.
4. An Annual Report on the World's Sustainable Development, culminating in a five-year address by the UN to the People of the planet. Each statement inclusive of the developmental priorities of the G8/G20 and legally binding all signatories to prepare for the next 5 years. This would become a new unifying action with leverage towards peaceful co-existence and mutual development for global civilization. For objective reasons, the key role in managing these processes of planetary integration must belong to the United Nations.

In the light of the above, our world needs a new strategy factoring in a necessary crisis response measures and mitigating threats to civilized life (the so called **New Policy**).

In order to form an ideological model for a step-by-step implementation, the following must be taken into consideration:

1. Up until 2020 we may expect to witness more crises in politics and the economy: not to mention turmoil on a local and global scale causing conflicts, wars and environmental calamities;

2. We are observing the advent of a new global multipolar system. Multipolarity will require a more equitable distribution of wealth between the nations and **a transformation of international institutions, such as the United Nations, the International Monetary Fund, the World Bank etc.**, which are currently dominated by the interests of already developed nations. Meaning, of course, the interests of emerging economies are under-represented. Hence, we must work to establish a global economy with minimal levels of risk and uncertainty;

3. The world today is in need of megaprojects designed to **improve the general standard of living**. Governments in industrialized countries, therefore, should go beyond narrow self-interest and begin to invest in programmes aimed at raising labour efficiency among **the world's poorest nations**.

4. Over the last few years geopolitical and socio-economic **forecasting** has been on the rise of global environmental and energy challenges, as well as a significant decline in food availability - caused by **growth in the world population**;

5. Humanity is now undergoing a global demographic revolution, which is characterized by an exponential growth in planetary population – soon to be replaced by **restricted reproduction**.

We are confident that **this new doctrine aims to further the development of global human society, based on ideals of morality and spirituality.** A call championed by the UN and discussed in future **UN Addresses to the World Population made every five years.** This will be a new step toward in understanding the evolutionary patterns of culture in the XXI century.

So, the United Nations will have a unique opportunity to regain its role (and mission) as a global unifying force - forming the core for **a new architecture of historical, moral, cultural, technological and environmental constructivism. Each aspect of which will be** founded on principles of justice, harmony and cooperation with every person on our Earth, along with the Cosmos itself. As such, it should be an institution fully accepting responsibility for the future evolution of human civilization. Overall, a revolutionary step in global security.

In order to test this proposed concept, it will be advisable to hold in 2018 a UN world conference for *"The New Strategy of World Development in the XXI Century"*. In such a context, it is urgent that the United Nations initiate a systematic analysis of the political, environmental, socio-economic order, so it may promptly work out common principles for the future development of our species: taking, thereby, immediate action regarding the pressing challenges of present day existence. In current conditions (characterized by high levels of uncertainty), we need to have at least a degree of confidence in our vision for tomorrow. **A view we authors believe should make a presentation before the relevant agencies of the UN: particularly UNESCO.**

All in all, this proposed megaproject may become the driving force to unite humankind. Another civilizational challenge for each member of humanity! Furthermore, world religions such as Islam, Judaism, Christianity, Hinduism and Buddhism should never endorse public discord or terrorism (the way they constantly appear in Western media), but rather urge unity, as well as promote high standards of ethics and security in global society. In other words, they should lead humanity forward in a moral revolution. **Thusly, this megaproject offers an ideological basis for developing global human society and establishing international security by leveraging high ethical standards and genuine technological progress.**

Proceeding from the statement above, I intend to address the UN, G8 and G20, during the annual Davos forum.

In summary, I want readers to note that I have always worked for humanity - with a view to making people safe and happy. If time confirms my intention, if the ideas of this project attract readers, if any of them influence improvements on their surroundings (or at least become aware of the transition to a type I Planetary civilization), I have not worked in vain. (**Figure 4**).

References for Chapter 3

1. 1.   Keynes. Return of the Master. - M.: JSC Yunayted Press, 2011.
2. 2.   Stiglitz J. Freefall: America, Free Markets and Sinking Economy Norton: 2009.
3. 3.   Yakovets Yu.V. Global Economic Transformations of XXI Century - M.: Economics, 2011.
4. 4.   Creative Capitalism. - M.: JSC Popurri, 2010.
5. 5.   The STIGLITZ REPORT – Reforming the International Monetary and Financial Systems in the Wake of Global Crisis. New York London.2010 .
6. 6.   Glazyev P.Yu. Sabden O., Armensky A.E., Naumov E.A. Intellectual economy – technological calls of XXI century. - Almaty: "Exclusive", 2009.
7. 7.   Glazyev P.Yu. Strategy of advancing development of Russia in conditions of global crisis. - M.: Economics, 2010.
8. 8.   Global economy and living arrangement on a threshold of new era. - M.: "Ankil", 2012.
9. 9.   Subetto A.I. The noosphere scientific and spiritual and moral bases of survival. Mankind in the XXI century. - SPB. : "Asterion", 2013.
10. 10.   Gleen J. Gordon T. Florescu E. State of the Future (The Millennium Project).2010 .
11. 11.   Kaku Michio. Physics of the future. - M, 2012.
12. 12 . Sabden O. Innovative economy. - Almaty: "Exclusive", 2008.
13. 13.   Moiseyev.N.M. Mankind – to be or not to be. - M.; 1999.

14. 14. Akayev A.A, Anufriyev I.E, Akayev B. A. The Vanguard Countries of World in the XXI Century in Conditions of Convergent Development. - M.: Book house "Librok", 2013
15. 15. Vernadsky V. I. Scientific thought as planetary phenomenon. - M.: Science, 1991.
16. 16. Russian newspaper. - 2004 / February 26 /
17. 17. Sadovnichy V.A. Akayev A.A. and others. Modeling and Forecasting of World Development. - M.: Moscow State University publishing house, 2012.
18. 18 .Shumpeter Y.A. Theory of economic development. M.: Direkt-media, 2007.
19. 19. Ricardo. D. Essentials to political economy and taxation. M.: EKSMO, 2007.
20. 20. Porter M. Competitive advantage. - M.: Alpine business of AXLE BOXES, 2008.
21. 21. SabdenO.ArmenskyA.Sustained economic growth in EurAsEC countries on the basis of laws of development. - Almaty, 2011.
22. 22. http: // en.wikipedia.org/wiki/Military – budget_ of_the_United_ \\\ States
23. 23. Friedman D. Next 100 years: forecast of XXI century events. - M.:Eksmo, 2010.

CHAPTER IV

Creatiing a new spiritual and technological cluster (Turkestan Valley) ways to humanize society

The know-how - without an analogue in the world. An international national megaproject. A pre-last gift to people and an international public. «Transformation of Turkestan into the Spiritual capital (center)» as a new step to ensuring international security. A new impulse to spiritual and technological development in the Republic of Kazakhstan during the XXI century.

(Representing a new world order is as essential as the "national idea" in previous ages. However, this new model unites West and East regions along the Great Silk way. As such, a new spiritual and technological development will occur within international security)

PREFACE

In the XXI century, the attention of our world civilization will focus on the east: towards "Big Asia" - including China, India, Russia and other countries. If we recall that the Great Silk way began in this region, it is possible to speculate on the special importance of this megaproject for our projected universal human civilization.

Nonetheless, the main purpose (not having analogues), of our undertaking is to evolve an International megaproject making Turkestan into the spiritual centre (megalopolis) of the region - thereby ensuring international security. So, for the first time in history, two cardinal problems have been connected i.e. the spiritual and historical elements of society, with new (V1 technological) methodologies showing Central Asia as an arena for Cultural Renaissance. All requiring an immediate practical conference devoted to this event.

The differences, of course, between present projects for technocratic (American style) developments - such as «Silicon Valley» - consists in having a coordinated spiritual and cultural design: along with a subsequently revived of tourism and appropriate infrastructures. Accordingly, these new requirements will rely on innovative V1 technological designs to empower its work for human benefit [1,2].

From the position of Turkestan, any movement of people, distribution of religions, ideas, cultures and arts, can only be strengthened through its original unity. Even though reliable sources about life in previous periods remains extremely limited. Be that as it may, various volumes sponsored by UNESCO have managed to incorporate the quintessence of long-term archaeological, orientalist and philosophical research to confirm the deep resources of this region. An area, which has held geopolitical significance for untold thousands of years.

So, at the international level «New Turkestan», in the XXI century, will be at the forefront of conflict resolution. Henceforth, its revival is not merely a recovery of a state territory, but rather a solution promising humankind the transformation of Eurasia into an integrative centre for international stability. Perhaps this is why Kazakhstan will declare itself a thoroughly denuclearized country, even though its uranium stocks are (arguably) the richest in the world. Undoubtedly, it is easy to envisage a "Baikonur spaceport", etc., along with other possibilities for indigenous nuclear power.

The most important thing –resulting from the management of uniform "processes coordination" in the spiritual-cultural development and innovative technological way, will be to provide an effective use of that most expensive capital – localized humanity. In this regard, Turkestan will concentrate the interests of about 400 million people. Such know-how becoming a new push for the whole world. In other words, in the XXI century, this progressive step towards a spiritual revolution bodes new forms of consciousness for humankind. After the realization of this megaproject, therefore, this consciousness-shift will transform the outlook of every regional model by its new spiritual and technological safety [3].

Confessedly, in this project we haven't tried to create something entirely new. On the contrary, along with the use of modern scientific technologies (re-born from our primordial ancient history and rich culture - we will remind fellow planetary citizens that European civilization was in those days considerably backwards: borrowing a lot of things from us), we will remind every Central Asia country of its greatness.

Indeed, in this manner, we have a unique historical opportunity through the "Turkestan onery" megaproject to return ourselves to the role of a global uniting centre. Exactly in the same manner we were in the days of the Great Silk way. Back then, an essential kernel of spirituality, a new architecture of cultural constructivism based on justice, harmony and cooperation, joined all the peoples of Eurasia. And as such, it is time to start this work again.

In the future, thanks to this regional Silk way project, there will be a possibility for creating «the card of a global way» - a safe development for the world. Thus, developing the thoughts of Vernadskiy farther (and looking to the future), we hope that the day will arrive when humankind reaches the cherished dream of using the space energy and resources of our solar system. At this point, we will be able to improve sustainable development for life on Earth. This is why we claim prominence should be given to noosphere-civilization [4].

Figure 4.1 ABOUT CREATION OF THE SPIRITUAL AND TECHNOLOGICAL CLUSTER «TURKESTAN ONERY»*

Purpose: To turn Turkestan into the spiritual center (megalopolis) of the international level. Revival of the Euroasian integration uniting the West and the East on the Great Silk way. Along with it, for the first time in history, on the example of one region to show to the world model of possibility of spiritual and cultural and new 6th technological innovative development of mankind.

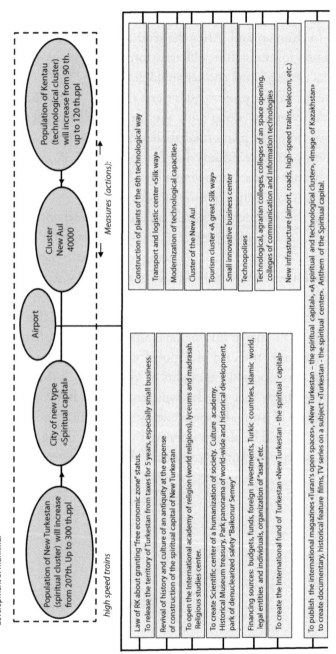

Population of New Turkestan (spiritual cluster) will increase from 207th. Up to 300 th.ppl

City of new type «Spiritual capital»

Airport

Cluster New Aul 40000

Population of Kentau (technological cluster) will increase from 90 th. up to 120 th.ppl

high speed trains

Measures (actions):

Construction of plants of the 6th technological way

Transport and logistic center «Silk way»

Modernization of technological capacities

Cluster of the New Aul

Tourism cluster «A great Silk way»

Small innovative business center

Technopolises

Technological, agrarian colleges, colleges of an space opening, colleges of communication and information technologies

New infrastructure (airport, roads, high-speed trains, telecom, etc.)

Law of RK about granting "free economic zone" status.

To release the territory of Turkestan from taxes for 5 years, especially small business.

Revival of history and culture of an antiquity at the expense of construction of the spiritual capital of New Turkestan

To open the International academy of religion (world religions), lyceums and madrasah. Religious studies center.

To create Scientific center of a humanization of society. Culture academy. Historical Museum treasury. Park panorama of world-wide and historical development, park of denuclearized safety "Baikonur Semey"

Financing sources: budgets, funds, foreign investments, Turkic countries, Islamic world, legal entities and individuals, organization of "asar", etc.

To create the International fund of Turkestan «New Turkestan «Turkestan - the spiritual capital»

To publish the international magazines «Turan's open spaces», «New Turkestan – the spiritual capital», «A spiritual and technological cluster», «Image of Kazakhstan» to create documentary, historical feature films, TV series on a subject «Turkestan - the spiritual center». Anthem of the Spiritual capital.

"difference of this project from "Silicon Valley" of the USA is in having coordinated spiritual and cultural development and aul revival, according to requirements of new time, with new innovational 6th technological way, to force it to work for the mankind benefit. After implementation of the new project «New Turkestan» it should be legally given the status of administrative area. At the international level «New Turkestan», uniting the West and the East, involving potential possibilities of the Great Silk way, becomes the century spiritual center.

Figure 4.2 Network model of International national mega project «New Turkestan»

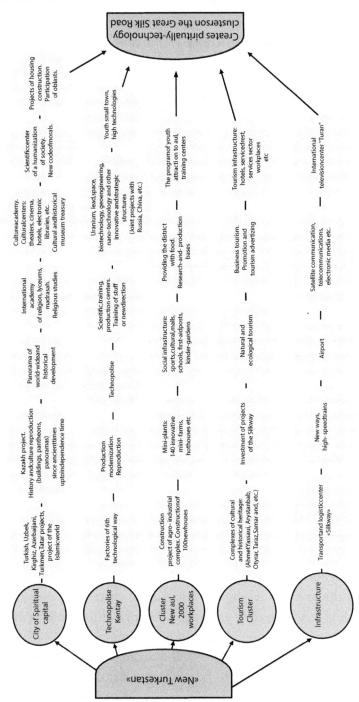

4.1 THE CONCEPT OF THIS PROJECT

Special importance and demand of the project

In what way are countries developing? How do we measure their development? Today our world is witnessing grandiose changes – world crises, global drowning, food shortages, hunger and other sorts of cataclysms leading to difficult political decisions. Similar changes, no doubt, have always influenced Society, as well as those who are at its wheel. Predetermining, possibly, mistrust in the future, along with any search for new ways to recover from each crisis [3].

Starting in 2008, a second wave of world crises seriously aggravated situations in the North American economy – not to mention the countries of Europe (Greece, Portugal, Spain, etc.). Each one experiencing financial difficulties and a complex cultural fallout. Nevertheless, healthy global competition usually strengthens recovery.

On reflection, however, natural cataclysms often entail numerous epidemics: every one engendering further concern for humankind [5]. And in such situations, many nation states experience flashes of upheaval. Our Kazakhstan being no exception. These secondary problems, therefore, have allowed spiritual degradation, universal corruption and idleness in local authorities (with their devil-may-care attitude to the needs of simple people) to became a catalyst for excess [6].

Sadly, bribery has become a scourge in our society. The problem of large-scale corruption (characterized by the surprisingly high levels of organization), proving hard to solve, while attempts to fight it never seem to yield results. Analogously, the religious situation in Kazakhstan has essentially fragmented: the number of religious associations (heterodox associations in 2011 exceeding 4500) steadily growing. Of course, this is subversive, since such religious trends are often dissonant and in opposition to general society – negatively influencing both youth and the senior generation [7]. A fact sharply showing state ideology to be ineffective before new developments.

So, in order for a state ideology to be respected, it is necessary to wisely choose the best methods to strengthen it.

This admitted, a number of states have chosen badly and simply follow the thoughtlessness of contemporary Westerners. As such, it is necessary to recall that current western ideology is primarily focused on consumption alone. The enrichment, dare one say, of small segments of the population. Similar to an infection (AIDS), therefore, the weakened state organism is finally undermined. Our Kazakhstan itself submitting to these dark influences. Thus, in the spiritual (mental) sphere (cinema, theatre, literature, music) Kazakhstan's citizens easily fall victim to mass media in its worst manifestations of violence, debauchery, self-interest, careerism, consumerism etc. To the extent that even inherited religion doesn't protect the population from moral decomposition and crime. All the aforementioned debilitating national security.

Unequivocally, our country is in the grip of social "diseases" originating from the industrialized countries, albeit without developing our own national "immunity". **Thusly, it is important to evolve a workable state ideology directed at preserving moral, cultural and traditional values.**

All meaning, Kazakhstan, while preserving its independence and place in the world community, still needs to strengthen its position. After all, towards the east, we border China (population about 1.5 billion people), to the north, Russia (50 million people), whilst to the south, we border India (about 1.2 billion) - factors which do not take into account the overwhelming American influence on our culture. So, in order to keep our independence, it is necessary to adhere to a multivector policy [8]. Integration into the global community, after all, is our right. Originally part of an association of regional states, these arrangements continue to suit Kazakhstan best. In which case, the development of large megaprojects, as well as their stage-by-stage realization, is an especially important task if we intend to increase the welfare of our population. Certainly, projects regarding territorial development raise the possibility of whole regions being strengthened immeasurably. The economic security of the state being in direct proportion to its advancement.

With this in mind, (pondering questions of crisis resolution), I came to the following conclusions. Firstly, the process of globalization should promote prosperity, although the clear enrichment of multinational companies is not the same thing. Indeed, at the beginning of the XXI century, this merely confuses the so-called "crisis web". Tellingly, millions of people live in penury: suffering from hunger and severe deprivations. A fact all advanced countries (G20, G8) claimed to oppose with a unanimous strategic plan. However, in recent years, they have gotten richer because of false value given to the US dollar: the volume of monetary weight exceeding the volume of made goods by 10-12 times. Under economic "law", it is doubtless that such violations of balance will lead to crisis after crisis. In many rich countries of the world, therefore, even new technological achievements are used only to increase capital for its own sake. Overall, a dangerous move.

In such a difficult situation, the United Nations, the International Monetary Fund, the European and the World development banks, the European union and other international financial and public organizations have proved helplessness. At the same time industrial and technological crises, III-IV-V-technological ways (TW), settled themselves. Hence, a new VITW is required, along with the formation and growth of a global economic masterplan for the world during the next decades.

Nightmarishly, when paying attention to other problems, we are simultaneously forgetting humanization at every turn: the perceived need to coexistence under Natural Law. Concomitantly then, society should always consider an organic adaptation like Nature itself. Yet, natural and human capital is hardly ever given paramount value. Instead, every law of harmonious development is broken, «the invisible hand of the market» serving to enrich already rich states, while taking the poor hostage.

The restoration of harmonious development in the XXI century, therefore, is only possible by limiting immediate returns, rather than encouraging endless production around finite material resources. New vision, new ideas, new projects of development, are needed - as opposed to old and tired techniques. Each one begging for innovative historical development.

As for the question what form should society take the XXI century, I consider two factors expedient:

First, a usage of logic for worldwide, historical, development, melded with primordial national history and the cultural values of each region.

Secondly, new views for the XXI century. We are transitioning to a post-industrial humanistic noosphere-civilization. Witnessing, as we are, the first stage of its outer adaptation - through new technological activities. As such, it is necessary to keep up to date with innovative technology and scientific research works [9].

Considering the foregoing, I shall put forward the following idea: «**Having coordinated together the spiritual and cultural aspects of humankind, as well as the 6th technological way, we must put into practice those uniform process which allow a transition towards harmonious development and sustainability. Following this ripening, we need to pass into a humanistic noosphere of integrated post-industrial advancement**».

Of course, the history of this new century isn't written yet. Nonetheless, cutting-edge knowledge and technological changes strongly suggest a world in transmutation. Thus, it is necessary to recognize that sometimes society doesn't manage to master those novelties promoting scientific progress. Admitted so, I present for your attention an addition to our proposed megaproject «**Turkestan Valley – a spiritual and technological cluster**». (In drawing 1 the purpose, structure, tasks etc. are shown)

This extra element adds a necessary second part

Initial direction: by means of spiritual and cultural revival, Turkestan will become a **spiritual centre**.

As an economic revival of the Great Silk way, attentive readers will recall that this transcontinental road connected European countries to those of the Far East. Noted so, in 2009 a highway from Western China to Western Europe (through Kazakhstan and the Russian Federation) was started. A cross-border project repeating the pattern of the Great Silk route. By 2015, it is hoped this road will be completely finished. From the very beginning of this process of globalization, therefore, the Great Silk way strangely joins antiquity to the future. Certainly, if we are discussing the INTERNET as a test case, the speediest method of information exchange, it demonstrates how ancient ideas can be used to empower modern thinking. Indeed, looking back, even in the Middle Ages, international merchant organizations agreed about prices, duties and trade transactions within conventional rules along the way. As such, the role of the Silk way was unique in the history of Eurasian peoples. So noted, its principal value is in the promotion of dialogue between cultures, uniting economies, and easing communication. Unsurprisingly then, the interest generated by this project led to talks discussing the possibility of preserving the Silk way as a listed world heritage site.

When studying old maps of Kazakhstan, we observe two ancient cities - Turkestan and Taraz. Historical data testifying that in the VI-VIII centuries, this territory was highly developed: being the Turkic khanate, wherein lived Turkic people. All meaning, ancient Turkestan had become a special place. Later, under the influence of historical processes, this Turkic khanate was broken up: an event dividing and dispersing these people to different corners of these territories. So, for example, Turks moved to Anadoliya, having formed the "Ottoman Empire", whereby (owing to the revolution organized by Kemal Ataturk), they became a separate state. Today, Turkey (with its population of 75 million people) is one of the most developed states in the G20.

Accordingly, my forecasts predict good fortune for Turkey. If it develops democratically – realizing the worth of its human capital - it will probably take a leading position in Europe, or even the world. Among Muslim countries, Turkey will certainly be in a premiere position by 2030.

But, despite past Turkic states, these peoples continue to consider Turkestan as their spiritual capital, calling it «Earth of fathers» (Atazhurt) and the second Mecca. Unarguably, crowds of pilgrims are flown to this city from all over the world each year to touch relics of the Holy Land: a living monastery of their fathers [10].

Stated so, our purpose is to turn Turkestan into a universal spiritual capital: a centre of culture, science and religion - developing it in accordance with XXI century requirements for Eurasian integration. Overall our addition to the original assertion of this megaproject. Hence, we need to realize the following (fig.1,2):

1) Pass in Parliament a new Law «New Turkestan–as a spiritual capital»;
2) Give New Turkestan the status of «a bonded economic area» and pass appropriate rules;
3) Release the territory of Turkestan (including Kentau city), from taxes for a period of 5 years, to allow small businesses to engage in trade;

All things considered, in Turkestan, the International Kazakh-Turkish university (founded by H.A.Yassavi) can function, along with top-level institutions such as an **«international academy of religion»** (world religions), a **«Cultural Academy»** and a **«Historical Museum treasury»**. Regarding **the humanization of society, this new Scientific centre will embrace the moral codes of XXI century life.** Understandably, the importance of this proposed new territory (our second Mecca) is that it will unite the spiritual, cultural, and religious heritage of Kazakhstan, along with every people in the Turkic world: a strategy **aiming at intellectual leadership**. These actions, of course, demand ideological works;

As agreed, between the cities of Turkestan and Kentau it will be necessary to construct a new spiritual capital. Albeit, on an architectural level, a town built on ancient Turkic lines - its colours, ornaments and motifs reflecting the region. Undeniably, Astana is the model of a capital city in the modernist style of our XXI century, yet Turkestan needs to become an example of collaboration between **Muslim peoples.**

Hence, in the spiritual capital it will be necessary to form «The international fund of Turkestan». To publish the Turanic editions of «New Turkestan– the spiritual capital», «A spiritual and technological cluster»,«Image of Kazakhstan» and create documentary and feature films;

Construction, this admitted, must involve the «Earth of fathers» (Atazhurt), as well as the peoples of Turkey, Uzbekistan, Azerbaijan, Turkmenistan, Kyrgyzstan and Tatarstan etc. Also, it is hoped all Islamic nations will offer a helping hand in this noble cause. Certainly, the restoration of historical monuments will compliment modern high-rise buildings. What is more, those visiting Turkestan should experience their culture through mausoleums and monuments.

Curiously, during the early stages of this project, my colleagues from Turkic-speaking countries said they would assist with the reconstruction of our ancient city. So, it is possible to rebuild pantheons to great historical figures in Turkic-speaking countries. From Tomiris, Atilla, Er tonba, Tonyyu and cook, to Arystanbab, Al - Farabi, Zhusip Balasagun, Manas, Nizami Gyanzhavi, Hodga Ahmet Yasaui, Kashgaria Makhmut, Beybarys Sultan, Emir Temir, Ulykbek, Alisher Nauayy, Muhammad Haidar Dulati, Korkyt, Abylay khan, Maktymgula, Abay Kunanbayev, Ataturk, Bektash Veli, Shokan Ualikhanov, Gabdolla Tokai, Mukhtar Auezov, Shyngys Aitmatov, Birdie Kerbabayev ..... and so on.

Tellingly, in this unstable century of globalization, the very idea of society's humanization becomes a factor in the unification of all peoples everywhere. After implementing the above, therefore, ample opportunities will present themselves for greater harmony between nations. Thereby, taking a big step towards futurity, while refusing to fall hostage to degradation. Thinking, in itself, adapting to new conditions.

4.2 CREATING CONCEPTUAL CLUSTERS FOR FUTHER DEVELOPMENT

Second direction. Undoubtedly, in the XXI century, globalization will strengthen. As such, Kazakhstan should evolve too. To our people, new technologies and innovative ways are vital. **Kazakhstan, thenceforth, should have a trajectory of accelerated development. This is why** I believe that it is possible (during the formation of the VI technological way) to develop biotechnology, nanotechnology, genetic engineering, electronic as well as information communication, not to mention the technology of space exploration, etc. Thusly, this second direction demands the following actions:

1) A consideration of new trends using human production capacities for the city of Kentau. Overall, it is necessary to **modernize** the capacities of the Kentausky excavator and transformer plants, JSCA chisay polimetall.

2) To construct **new plants in the VI technological way**. Prepare, in other words, a hi-tech staff for the new directions. To open a park devoted to a denuclearized world "Baikonur Semey".

3) It is necessary to construct **a transport and logistic centre «Silk way» (Zhibek-Zholy), a small innovative business centre (a technopolis), a technological college and other infrastructures.** Phrased differently, it is essential **to create a new technological cluster**. In which case, constructing a spiritual centre, while equally creating - in Kentau - bases for the new VI technological way. Each development thereby creating an innovative **spiritual and technological cluster** in our country.

4) Indeed, throughout the Great Silk way, it is necessary **to develop tourism clusters**. A programme designed to generate mono-cities.

5) **A cluster creation of Auls to set an example of sustainability**. This cluster will give exact answers to what XXI century Kazakhaul will be like. Some planners saying, the development of these auls will promote our country. Thus, «a cluster of Auls» will encourage the building of new workplaces, stop the leakage of youth to cities, as well as solve the problem of demography-shift. Assuredly, this project will be an embodiment of a centuries-old ancestral dream: especially affecting **natural processes of demographic take-off.** A problem, of course, becoming a priority. **Clearly, without an increased number of young people, we won't become a rich, powerful, state**.

6) Thenceforth, our Eurasian megaproject will strengthen its geopolitical value by attracting China, Russia, Turkey and other countries into greater collaboration. Also, it will attract investors from these states to sponsor space exploration (Baikonur), tourism and logistical building long the «Great Silk way». All encouraging the construction of

plants using new technologies, the application of uranium and other resources for regional peace.

4.3 AN ADDITIONAL JUSTIFICATION

At the heart of such a large project is the reconstruction of two cities- Turkestan and Kentau- both designed to pioneer new models of spiritual, cultural and technological development. Herein, the spiritual and cultural branches meld with components of the new XI technological way. Argued so, we will work for a radical humanization of our world. Only spiritual and technological constructivism will give humankind a chance to solve age-old dislocations in our culture. This megaproject's implementation, therefore, enables a functioning alternative to current urban development to establish **new models of a humanization in society. As such, this starts a new age new of enculturation.**

In this regard, it is necessary to hold an international scientific and practical conference and project presentation at a global level. After all, problems of this sort haven't yet been solved in such a systematic form [6].

Equally considered, around "Big Turkestan" are many Central Asia countries (about about 400 million people can be involved in this idea) forming a huge workforce. Former errors, no doubt, will slow any technological surge (a technokratizm), yet our humanistic purposes were not previously taken into account because of absence of spiritual and technological constructivism.

Moreover, the difference between this project from **"SiliconValley"** in the USA is that humankind itself benefits, i.e. one solution being an aul revival together with new innovative technologies. The huge territory of Turkestan in the centre of Central Asia linking its development with the movement of people, the distributions of religions and fresh ideas, cultures and arts etc. UNESCO reports confirming that researches by archaeologists, orientalists and philosophers agree about the unending capacity of our region.

This new megalopolis and its vicinities will house 300 thousand people, while the city of Kentau about 150 thousand people. In the future - between the cities of Turkestan and Kentauin - the new spiritual capital will house more than 100 thousand people. In addition, the southern regions (in cities like - Shymkent, Taraz, Kyzylorda, Almaty) will live more than 7,9 million people [11]. Possibly, making this the most densely populated region wherein ethnic Kazakhs are concentrated. Undoubtedly, the influence of such immense human potential (in aggregate with all the population of Kazakhstan) opens unsuspected doorways.

As was already noted, this region is located along the Great Silk way, with locations such as Otrar listed by UNESCO. Herein, we find Hodzhi Ahmed Yasavi's mausoleum, seldom photographed, the burial site of the ancient saks "Golden Man" (Esik), Aksu- Dzhabagla fully preserved and other archaeological excavations. All of which have become a brand for our country amid foreign tourists [10]. So, the creation of a **cluster for international tourism** in the spiritual and cultural capital is essential.

4.4 FINANCING SOURCES

Financing sources (justification):

1. The state, republican, local budgets within the law: use of means of the RK National fund.
2. With a view towards the revival of the transformative cradle of the Turkic world in Turkestan as a spiritual capital «**The international fund**».
3. Attracting foreign investments into innovative, new technological projects.
4. Rendering support by Turkic countries regarding the revived lands of their fathers (Atazhurt) as the Spiritual capital. There is hope, because Islamic countries will participate in this project. The new Spiritual capital will gain completely new links.

5. Each area will bring contributors to this project. To create a pantheon of celebrated personalities from Kazakh history, along with a martial panorama of great battles and acts of courage.
6. Financing this project will necessitate funds from corporate and legal entities. Asar and other actions will be organized.

Any realization of this Spiritual and technological Cluster «the Turkestan Valley» is transferrable to the jurisdiction of the Government and international investors - put under Parliamentary control. To maintain the international image of this project designated officers **under the patronage of the President of our RK** need to be employed.

The special value of this project is found in its coordination of spiritual, cultural, scientific and technological structures working in uniform process – as well as the rational management of its results in terms of potential-human interaction. As such, a unanimous decision about the megalopolis project needs encouraging. **Today, our world must focus on civilized development: a spiritual and technological centre, that is:**

1) Ancient Turkestan - should become the humanized spiritual centre of global society. Reviving, thereby, a cultural wealth of nationalities from many states. Thus, there will be a force able to unite the people of our country in new ways.
2) The cities centres must soften these new technological clusters: transport and logistic clusters, a spirituality cluster and clusters of auls for tourism – will all give an impulse towards innovative development.
3) In this region, the spiritual capital will have an eastern style. Each area, each ethnos, will see a reflection of indigenous culture, history, customs and traditions. As such, New Turkestan will make changes to human consciousness.
4) The power of this territory will be defined by two factors: an enriched capital and its Eurasian geographical arrangements. Hence, ending in 2015, the construction of a road between Western China and Europe - will restore the Great Silk way. Its capacity and efficiency being more efficient

than ocean voyages, or maritime routes. In terms of resource-richness Kazakhstan takes 9th place in oil production, whereas, in uranium, the 1st one. Their effective development is our great goal.

Especially today, statements by the English scientist and politician, (an outstanding scholar in geopolitics) Ch. D. Makkinder, remind us, «The country supervising Eurasia – supervises also the whole world» [13]. A statement actually asking if domination comes from the seas or land? Now, land monitoring differs from monitoring waters in that it is more demanding. After all, untold millions of people live on land. If, therefore, Genghis Khan in the XI century had died from a sword and a spear, we Kazakhs would not need a new project – neither would the world around us. So, this megaproject is presented as a scientific exploration (potential know-how), into reliable international security. It is possible to say we have made an unexpected find (of a brilliant idea), so to speak, of a discovery in a new vector of development. As such, this spiritual and technological project examines general strategy on every level.

In summary, it is desirable to note that any realization of this international/national megaproject «Transformation of Turkestan into the spiritual capital» will allow not only an increase of prestige amongst Kazakh people, but also encourage a new form of pride amid Muslim states. **Today, this project should become a motive power uniting all. It will be a new call to civilization across the whole world: especially in rich countries!** In other words, it is a fearless step towards a genuine revolution in consciousness. **So, this megaproject becomes a regional model for new spiritual and technological advances leading to international security.**

After the implementation of this new project, of course, the district «New Turkestan» must legally be given the status of an administrative area. At the international level «new Turkestan» would become the spiritual centre wherein the West and the East promote integration, involving possible interactions along the Great Silk way [14].

New Turkestan, having a zone of influence, **will turn into the Eurasian integration centre –a place of cultural wealth for many countries.**

Furthermore, the sustainable development of Kazakhstan will be probable at this point. As soon as this regional project yields results, an agenda for ideal development has been established. Probably evolving under the aegis of the United Nations – with the assistance of UNESCO.

At the end of the day, Kazakhstan aspires to nuclear safety and calls other countries into peaceful co-existence. Our denuclearized state - being the largest country in the region - playing an appreciable role in providing both state, and regional security. Thusly, Kazakhstan makes an enormous contribution to universal civilization.

Table 1 Financial and Economic Calculations of The Megaproject

1. Project «NewTurkestan»			Mln. dollars
1.1	City of the Spiritual capital		590
	1.1.1	Turkish, Uzbek, Kirghiz, Azerbaijani, Turkmen, Tatar projects, project of the Islamic world of the VI-XXI centuries	700,0
	1.1.2.	Kazakh project. History and culture reproduction (buildings, pantheons, panoramas) since ancient times and finding independence	100,0
	1.1.3.	International academy of religion, lyceums, madrasah. Religious study centres.	100,0
	1.1.4.	Culture academy. Cultural centers: theatres, cinemas, hotels, electronic libraries, etc. Cultural and historical museums, treasury.	250,0
	1.1.5.	Scientific center for the humanization of society. New code of morals.	70,0
	1.1.6.	Projects of housing construction. Participation in areas	300,0
1.2.	Kentau's technological cluster		1 245,0
	1.2.1.	Plants of the VI technological way	450,0
	1.2.2.	Production modernization. Reproduction	25,0
	1.2.3.	Technopolises	120,0
	1.2.4.	Scientific,training, production centres. Training for the new direction.	50,0

	1.2.5.	Uranium, lead, space, biotechnology, a geninzheneriya, a nanotechnology, etc. innovative and strategic structures (Joint projects with Russia, China, etc.)	200,0
	1.2.6.	Youth small town, high technologies	400,0
1.3	**Cluster NewAul of 2000 labours**		**850,5**
	1.3.1.	Construction project of agro-industrial complex. Construction of 100 new houses	400,0
	1.3.2.	Mini-plants: 140 innovative mini-farms, hothouses etc.	180,0
	1.3.3.	Social infrastructure: sports, cultural, malls, schools, first-aid posts, kindergartens	220,0
	1.3.4.	Providing district food. Research-and- production bases	50,0
	1.3.5.	The programme of attraction for youth in an aul, training centre	0,5
1.4.	**Cluster of Tourism**		**113,0**
	1.4.1.	Complexes of cultural and historical heritage: (AhmetYassaui,Arystanbab, Otyrar,Taraz, Samarkand, etc.)	3,0
	1.4.2.	Investment of Silk way projects	25,0
	1.4.3.	Natural and ecological tourism	5,0
	1.4.4.	Business tourism. Promotion and advertizing of tourism	10,0
	1.4.5.	Tourism infrastructure: hotels, service rest. Services sector workplaces etc.	70,0
1.5.	**Infrastructure**		**4 310,0**
	1.5.1.	Transport and logistic center «Silk way»	440,0
	1.5.2.	New ways, high-speed trains	850,0
	1.5.3.	Airport	1 800,0
	1.5.4.	Satellite communication, telecommunications, electronic media, etc.	220,0
	1.5.5.	International television centre «Turan»	1 000,0
2 Project presentation. Carrying out the international scientific and practical conference, business of forums.			0,5
			8 039,0

References for Chapter 4

1. D. Friedman The Next 100Years: A Forecast of events of the XXI century. - M.: Penguin Books,2010.
2. SabdenO.Kogamdyizgilendirumenkauipsizdik-Zhanaalemdiktərtiptinnegizi. Almaty:Kazakh University, 2013.
3. Sabden O. humanization of society and security- the basis of the new world order. Almaty: KazakhUniversity,2013.
4. Vernadsky V.I. Scientific thought as a planetary phenomenon.- Moscow: Nauka, 1991.
5. Michio Kaku. Physics of the future.- M.,2012.
6. S   a   b   d   e   n O.XXIFasyrdaFyadamzattynOmirsYrustrategiyasynynkontseptsiyasy, Almaty: KRBGMGKIE, 2014.
7. Lama Sharif. Kazakhstan Today. -August 10. In 2011.
8. T.Mansurov Eurasian project, Nursultan Nazarbayev, embodied in life.- M.: Real-Press, 2014.
9. Sabden O.A new global outlook and a model of the world order. –Almaty Aytumar, 2013.
10. Baipakov KM, Azimhan A. All roads lead to Turkestan: monuments person-Almaty,2013.
11. Regions of Kazakhstan (stat. sbornik). - Astana, 2013.
12. N. A Nazarbayev Address to the People of Kazakhstan: Kazakhstan Today. -17.01.2014.
13. Mackinder H.S. Democratic ideals and reality.- New York: Holt,1919.
14. Social values, Science and Technology (Eng) (pdf). European Commission P / 7-11 / Europa portal (june2005).Arihivirovano from the original on21 August 2011.

REVIEW

Of the megaproject by O. Sabden*«A construction of strategies for human survival in the twenty-first and subsequent centuries»*

Almaty, LLP «FreshIdeas»2014, p.42.

Originally, this scientific concept (and methodology) for the construction of a "planetary home" for human civilization in a post-industrial world was developed by an academician from the Republic of Kazakhstan O. Sabden. In contrast to narrowly focused approaches, the main point of Professor O. Sabden was to show that the transition to a post-industrial civilization must be based on a comprehensive and systematic study of the problems of world development - along with a proposal for specific mechanisms and their practical implementation.

Thus, the idea of this author is centred on the combination of a number (six) of key elements allowing, in his opinion, future generations to build a productive (regulating) system of global processes. Thereby making, on that basis, the right decisions for worldwide progress. In this context, the author suggests creating a world legislature (World Parliament), an executive body (world government), a judicial authority (World Court), a Security Council and a council of wise men from across the world.

As an academician of the Republic of Kazakhstan, O. Sabden also suggests we create (within the framework of integration), a single world currency regulator, along with a single world currency union: cross-currency reserves and a set threshold to ensure global security.

Overall, the author sees his proposed global system of control (and the regulation of global processes) in the form of a mathematical model, but without specifying its type or basic properties.

It is unclear, therefore, what the real mechanisms for this global network would be, or how one may ensure its smooth functioning - both in terms of an operational and civilized resolution to potential conflicts: let along from the point of view of the sources of its continuous funding. Now, the enthusiasm of Professor O. Sabden deserves our respect. He is a prominent Kazakh scientists, after all, who seeks to solve complex (both in formulation and in their implementation) global problems. Moreover, his unwavering belief in the ability of modern science at its present stage of development, along with the current level of maturity amongst the international community (torn by intractable contradictions of principle) speaks volumes about his personal integrity. Quite apart from his belief in humanities ability to resolve the most complex socio-economic issues.

Nevertheless, in the above context, I wish this project "A construction of strategies for human survival in the twenty-first and subsequent centuries," - and its author (doctor of economic sciences, academician of Kazakhstan, President of the

Union of Scientists of Kazakhstan, State Prize winner, Orazaly Sabden - every success in its implementation. Indeed, I would consider it as an honour to be of benefit to the author and his work.

*Overall, I am sure that in the case of this proposed solution the author, academician O.Sabden, **deserves** the very highest global awards.*

Academician of the Washington Academy of Sciences,
Co-winner of the Nobel Peace Prize

Timashev S.A.

22 June 2014

SECTION **II**

ENSURING FOOD SAFETY

CHAPTER V

International Problems with Food Security

C urrently, humanity is confronting dangers, the most pressing of which are food, energy and the environment. All generating a complicated global picture. Now, the volumes of energy consumption and the alleged consumption of hydrocarbon fuels have significantly increased due to technological progress and better agricultural production. Yet, the subsequent release of greenhouse gases into our biosphere threatens the environment through climate change, melting glaciers, rising sea levels and soil degradation. Never forgetting, of course, the high rate of population growth and the sharp reduction of basic resources such as arable land and fresh water supplies. Indeed, the rising costs of energy needed for agricultural production are staggering. For example, the International Food and Agriculture Organization (FAO) has documented the annual disappearance of 7 million hectares of arable land. A fact compounded by 1 billion 300 million undernourished people (more than 180 million children). In Africa, sadly, there are 175 million people living "without sufficient food". By 2010, their number will have increased to 300 million. Currently, more than 6 billion people struggle for survival: an annual population growth of 92-93million. Hence, the International Institute for Systems Analysis in Austria predicted that by 2030 the total population of our Earth will be 9.5 billion. According to their calculations, the second half of the XXI century will witness a population of 12 billion. Meanwhile, America and Europe has more than 20 million hectares of arable land, while in Africa it is about 80 million. Yet, with an annual disappearance of about 7 million hectares of arable land, this is little consolation. In many countries, therefore, no further development is possible. So stated, in Nepal slopes - and those of the Philippine – along with the slopes of active volcanoes farming is undertaken. Although, in Brazil, whole forests are being burnt: rapidly depleting already poor soils. In the arid regions of India, nonetheless, intensive irrigation leads to salinization. So, the contradictions between agricultural use and environmental protection are intensifying every day.

Per capita production, of course, gives a true picture of available food. In 1950, there was 247 kg of grain per person, while in 1984 it was 346 kg. According to various estimates, this noted, the amount of grain will not be enough for minimum global needs in about 30-40 years.

In order to meet growing demands, there must be 100 to 200 million hectares of arable land worldwide - according to UN data. Simultaneously, statistics show there is a continuous reduction in the volume of agricultural products. In the 1980s, the average annual growth of food (worldwide) was 30 million tons. However, in the last 20 years, only 12 million tons were on the market: estimates suggesting a further decline to 9 million tons by 2030. Even though, the population by that time will have increased to 8.9 billion people.

So, the International Grains Council (IGC) in 2007, collected 1.568 billion tons of grain, while in 2006, they gathered 1.612 billion tons: a reduction in the world's reserves from 315 million to 282 million tons. Yet, if the biofuels industry (from corn) increases at the same pace, the need for grain will grow by 2.5 times. Despite the fact that the level of GDP per rural resident in agriculture in Kazakhstan is 1.8 times lower than in Russia – wherein it is 7.5 times higher than in Germany or South Korea. Furthermore, in Central Asia, there are 150 species of pests, 120 species of weed and 70 types of diseases, which in turn equally reduces the efficiency of agriculture. Additionally, these natural factors have a negative effect through poor scientific methods and disorganized management. Therefore, the following is noticeable:

- The low level of entrepreneurial culture using new technology;
- The lack of an effective system of incentives for the introduction of new scientific developments into production;

– Unattractiveness of research work for highly qualified personnel and young scientists;
– The lack of effective mechanisms, or good practices, for cooperation between innovators;
– In adequate integration of domestic science;
– Old scientific, technical and material resources;
– The lack of engineering companies transferring knowledge, or scientific and technological experience, in production.

Perhaps in response to such issues a global food security programme was adopted by the "Group of Eight" on July 8th, 2008, in Japan (Hokkaido, Toyako Onsen). A decision welcomed by the Heads of State «G8" when they said: "We are deeply concerned that the sharp rise in food prices across the world - in conjunction with existing problems in a number of developing countries concerning the food supply - is threatening global food security. The negative effects of this trend occurring recently could plunge millions more people into poverty, or reverse any progress in achieving Millennium Development Goals"».

What is the way out of this disastrous situation? Surely not those chemicals used in agriculture that have already exhausted their palliative possibilities. Indeed, this field needs a fundamentally new scientific approach - with solutions based on the latest achievements of science and alternative energy. In our opinion, the solution is informational. Asserted so, the definition adopted by the UNESCO, information technology group (IT) seems applicable. Particularly when we recall they are suggesting a set of interrelated, scientific and technological disciplines be applied to effectively organize people's labour through information processing and storage. Thinking outside the box, they add organizational methods, production equipment and its praxis will solve social, economic and other cultural ills. The purpose of any information technology, after all, being to get the required information to a given carrier.

As a case in point, internationally, there are different methods of pre-plant treatment for seeds and tuber crops. Some advocating chemical treatments encouraging growth through coating plants with organic-mineral mixtures. Others, championing bio-stimulation through electric and magnetic fields, ultraviolet and microwave radiation, ionizing radiation, plasma treatments, and so on. These latter techniques made more efficient, arguably, due to the huge proportion of manual labour. Tellingly, this admitted, chemical treatments and the heavy application of pesticides during the process of fertilization and weed control, both pollute the environment and causes irreversible damage to the soil microflora: causing, thereby, changes to the genetic code in plants, humans and animals. Along with an increasing frequency of mutations and human cancers, hereditary diseases etc.

Now, the theory of weak ripple effects through electromagnetic fields on biological objects was developed by A.Chizhevsky, V.I.Vernadsky, N.A.Kozyrev and a researcher of cosmogeophysical relationships S.E. Schnol. The result being that a new concept of "Unity of the fundamental properties of biopolymers functioning" and the new science of "Synergy", which is closely related to biological phenomena and objects in the environment, was founded.

Curiously, even small fluctuations within interplanetary magnetic fields may be responsible for significant changes to climate, the biosphere and the physiology of animals as well as plants, on Earth. In this context, therefore, the problem of solar-terrestrial relations, or more recently, correlations between Cosmo-physical terrestrial processes, have attracted the attention of researchers. The phenomenon of electromagnetic fields on biological objects being grasped as an exchange of energy information in nature.

Additionally, innovative technologies have recently confirmed that the biorhythms of agricultural crops are affected. These technologies, of course, include finings on the influence of natural gravitational and artificial electromagnetic fields. The key feature of these technologies being to synchronize the effects of these fluctuations with the geomagnetic field (at a given point) of the Earth. What is more, emissions from near and far space, along with the biorhythms of the objects in question, read like inter-globular conversions [1]

Astoundingly, the systematic influence of gravitational fields from the Sun, Moon, Earth and other planets in our solar system affects all life. Also, the influence of electromagnetic fields, periodically generated by the sun, as well as additional artificial electromagnetic radiation (that has the same electromagnetic frequency as biorhythms in the seeds) obviously interacts with the biorhythms of plants. All making researchers think in new directions.

As a result, this type of celestial impact on the metabolism of cells inside plants moves them to a higher energy level of biological activity. All allowing reliable confirmation that an increase in the activity of alpha and beta-amylase, coupled with the hydrolysis of starch and dextrin endosperm to oligo-, di- and monosaccharides permits a greater consumption of food by seedlings and the roots of plants. Indeed, the synthesis of gibberellin increases in the embryo - as a result of which the development of the root system accelerates. All concluded by the vigorous germination and rapid transition to an autotrophic type of food that the plant requires to form a strong photosynthetic apparatus.

Researchers defending the positive effect of various electromagnetic (or any informational radiation on the productivity of plants) have long been named. For example, G. Lakhovsky is considered a pioneer in these studies (born in 1870 in Russia and died in 1942 in the USA). Interestingly, it was G. Lakhovsky who came to the following three assumptions after numerous experiments of his own, not to mention those by European scientists:

1. Life originates through radiation.
2. Life is supported through radiation.
3. Life is destroyed through radiation.

Accordingly, for G. Lakhovsky, living cells are small oscillatory circuits that emit ultrashort electromagnetic waves. Stars also emit these same waves. Thus, due to the resonance between cellular and stellar waves, the relationship of life processes on Earth and those processes that occur in space are starting to be established.

Additionally, in 1930, A.G. Gurevich found out that the bio-field plays a role as the programme-carrier of morphological developments in plants. At the end of the XX century, moreover, P.P. Goryaev discovered the existence of a genome wave, which is the frequency-wave component of DNA (its primary information programme).

Unexpectedly, a researcher of Chinese origin from Khabarovsk, Jiang Kanchzhen, proved in practice that the transfer of an information programme, or bio-field, between one organism and another is possible by means of electromagnetic waves at ultrahigh frequencies. Amazingly, he also found that the human biological field emits a microwave spectrum. In order to demonstrate his assumption, he created a lens that can focus this radiation, or strengthen it. As such, these concentrated bio-waves can activate the so-called silent genes (their quantity in organisms is up to 95-99%) demonstrating, somewhat strangely, that these genes do not age. When they are "awake", they synthesize proteins allowing them to "self-restore" any damage in existing cells.

Finally, the Moscow physicists G.I. Shipov and A.E. Akimov, after the completion of numerous studies in torsion fields, came to the conclusion that a revolutionary future in the fields of energy, environmental and agricultural technology, will belong to the torsion component of information.

Sadly, these studies, confirmed by DNA results and general frequency-wave programmes in plants and living organisms (i.e. the existence of a primary informational programme) have yet to reach general audiences. In this regard, however, research on the positive influence of electromagnetic fields (low frequency, high frequency, laser and other processing), or the enhancement of informational programmes on plant materials, will improve the productivity of crops worldwide.

THE SELENIUM-, SOLAR- AND CHRONOBIOLOGY

Philosophical works, treatises, books and articles concerning the affects of the Moon on Man are numerous and largely belong to the ancient period. Clearly, some of the earliest information on these interactions going back to the days of Aristotle, Plutarch, Hippocrates, Galen and Paracelsus [2].

Provocatively, it appears all cultures in our world have myths, legends and beliefs claiming good health is associated with the influence of the Moon and its phases. Cyclic changes of the Moon being said to hold great importance for the human body. As such, it is totally unjustifiable to deny the experience of endless centuries of observation: rejecting these nuggets of knowledge as primitive speculation, or conclude they are mere superstition.

An ongoing interest in this issue (supported by the practicalities of everyday life), therefore, indicates that behind these assertion there is a real linkage. Albeit, one proving difficult to identify. Undoubtedly, information about the role of the moon in human affairs was documented in ancient manuscripts that cannot be unconditionally taken for granted. However, at the same time, they cannot be rejected without scrutiny - for they retain the hard won memory, experience, and wisdom garnered over thousands of years. Thus, it would be correct to say, "Precious nuggets of ancient intuitive knowledge are now confirmed by the boldest hypotheses of our time". [3]

Of course, modern data on the influence of the moon on biological systems are already in the scientific literature of different countries. One of the most extensive monographs ever written being in Swedish [4]. In addition, German researchers have repeatedly discussed these problems [5-6], while a number of great review papers on the medical aspects of the Moons influence have been published in English and American literature [7-9].

So stated, fascinating original information on "selenobiology" and "seleno-medicine" is outlined in a book written by M. Dubrov [10]. A work debating the hypothesis that a biological role, along with a power over tidal flows, is manifestly evident. Yet, the suggestion of a "biological tide" - based on the assumption that biological systems are also subjected to the same influence of gravitational forces – takes thinking into our modern era. Even though, this acknowledged, contemporary researchers have shown [11] it is a very simplified way of analyzing gravitational fields and distant influences. Nonetheless, water in biological systems is not as free as in the oceans and seas. Rather, it is closely linked with hydrophilic bonds, with biomolecules, ions, organic molecules and various complex compounds with cell membranes and cellular organelles. Although, this claimed, even in the "free" water of the oceans and seas, tides vary greatly in their nature: due to various physical factors (topography, coastline, coastal depths, square bodies of water, prevailing currents, etc.). So, the force of the Moon, or the Sun, must manifests in a radically different form in organisms. Be that as it may, the gravitational influence of the Sun and Moon affects all spheres of Earth - air, water and land, despite the vast distances separating them. Revealing, probably, that the concept of gravity as a physical factor was only agreed as an agent in the middle of the XVII century: when the great physicist Isaac Newton coined the term. Thereafter, obscuring studies by scientists from different countries undertaken in the XIX and XX centuries (on the physical basis of gravitation), who felt the force of the Moon and Sun needed to become clearer. Debates impacting academia, both directly and indirectly, in a number of diverse ways. [12] Obviously, however, the most significant of these phenomenon are the oceanic tides. Differing, as they do, in scope and amplitude across various geographical areas [13]

Noted so, people have watched tides throughout the ages and were convinced of their connection to lunar phases! Furthermore, these centuries-old observations led some scholars to speculate about their effect on human fertility, the ozone layer, geomagnetic activity and rainfall [14]. "Our study of the Moon, our future, may depend largely on a better understanding of the Moons influence on Earth" [15]. Possibly, the most interesting discussion centres around grand-scale processes covering the entire Earth. Assuredly, Earth's shell is moulded by insignificant variations of gravity. Weirdly, therefore, lunar-solar attractions on bodyweight (for example, 1 ton varies by only 0.2 grams) generates important questions. When all said and done, the magnitude in gravitational change can be judged from the following figures: any acceleration due to the gravity of the Earth being equal to 982.04 cm/s^2 (g = 982,04 gallons), while the maximum variation due to the influence of the Moon and Sun is only 240.28 micro gals (or 0 24 milligal). Phrased differently, to one hundred thousandth of a percent of the "G". Additionally, 164.52 milligal comes from the action of the Moon and 75.76 mg per share of the gravitational influence from the Sun. These "insignificant" magnitudes of gravitational force are sufficient, of course, to drive the continuous movement of billions of tons of water, earth, and the expanse of air masses.

Explained so, the tides are created by the joint action of gravity from the Moon and Sun on our Earth. The biggest impact being from the Moon, since (even though it is disproportionately small in comparison to the size of the Sun), the Moon is closer to Earth. Yet, the relative positions of Earth, Moon and Sun are always changing. In which case, the magnitude of the tides also changes. Hence, the tides hit maximum during the New Moon, while during a Full Moon - when the Moon and the Sun are located in one straight line to the Earth – they recede. Minimum tides are called quadrature (from the Latin word "Area" - a quarter). Each process observed in the phase of the first and last quarter of the moon, when the difference between the coordinates of the Moon and Sun is 90°, i.e. when they are at right angles. Terrestrial and atmospheric tides are less known [16]. After all, they are not as obvious as the oceanic sea, but they equally have a global dimension. For instance, in the upper mantle of the Earth, where the outermost shell of the Earth's crust is located, the attractive force of the Moon and Sun causes a periodic rising and lowering of the surface: as recorded by gravimeters, or measured through localized changes in gravity. Under the influence of the Moon, the Earth's surface rises to a maximum of 35.6 cm and lowers to 17.8 cm, while the Sun, respectively, influences surface vibrations up to 16.4 cm and down to 8.2 cm. The total effect of these lunar-solar oscillations of the earth's surface being 78 cm: under the influence of the moon - 53.4 cm, while it is 24.6 cm under the influence of the Sun. This is a kind of "breathing" for the Earth - the movement of its surface under the influence of gravitational forces. As claimed above, these grandiose progresses of aquatic and terrestrial layers are influenced by those gravitational forces making up the vast proportion of the earth's gravity module. Certainly, the continuous movement of the earth's surface leads to large changes in the structure of the Earth's crust, the Earth's rotation around its axis, the orbital parameters of motion and other geophysical phenomena (in particular, continental drift, the shift of oceanic plates and even an increase in the frequency of earthquakes) [17].

Additionally, there are large-scale changes in the atmosphere enhanced by periodic heating from the Sun under the influence of the gravitational effects of the Moon and Sun. Changing air pressure being an indicator of atmospheric tides. Now, tidal power arising from the gravitational influence of the Moon and Sun is constantly changing due to the rotation of our planet and other factors. However, the very characteristic waves of our world are stored during the day: only latterly being transformed in shape and amplitude - depending on the geographic latitude. Clearly, the structure of this wave has two main components - lunar and solar. Considered so, we have studied the effect of these tidal forces of the Moon on the Earth's biological processes: in particular, on the optimal time for the treatment of seeds. The question of their exposure to electromagnetic fields at low frequencies plays, this confessed, an important role in the overall issue of the impact of electromagnetic fields on living systems. Its relevance, of course, determined by the fact this area includes the frequency of electromagnetic fields in power lines in a variety of industrial applications and home appliances, as well as the frequency of geomagnetic and Cosmo-physical fluctuations [21-22].

Models of those mechanisms acting on ultra-weak factors in biological systems remain revealing [23], based, as they are, on the fact that every living system has an intermolecular aqueous medium, which is the initiator of structural organization of the two. As such, researchers have contended 1) the structural organization of water - as a condensed phase of matter, H_2O, contains its own clusters and catharses built around organic and inorganic contaminants. Each one mixed with the structural elements of water (OH + -O) - to (OH) PNP's [24]; 2) and the structural organization of water adjacent to the biomolecules initiating energy transfers in the processes of living systems. This structural organization is itself created by periodic passages of "polarization waves" generated by the processes of energy storage: especially in the form of solitons as they move along the various chains of macromolecules. This conclusion is founded on the soliton theory of A. Davydov [25] and the "polarization approach" of G. Frelih [26].

It goes without saying there are works in which the stimulatory effects of low-frequency electromagnetic fields (low EMF) on seeds [27] have been investigated. It was found, curiously, that the germination of seeds was stimulated under the influence of LF EMF – depending, of course, on the degree of membranes stretched when they were swollen [28]. It was also observed that a long-term exposure to EMF (during seed imbibition) leads not only to growth inhibition among seedlings, but equally to a drop in their germination. It binds, one might say, to the desynchronization of growth by stimulating the release - and inhibition - of protein bonding. Therefore, any proposed physico-chemical mechanism explaining the main features of EMF ow impacts on organisms, must include a sensitivity towards magnetic storms and their weakening effects, along with the increasing amplitude of EMF.

An important indicator of the sensitivity of biological system to geophysical factors is magnetic susceptibility [29]. Regardless of the type of plant, at sunrise the magnetic susceptibility in leaves is increased, it reaches maximum at noon, drops in the afternoon, and falls to a minimum at night. Although, around 3-4am, during the pre-dawn hours, it again reaches the initial level from which to make any count.

In our work, we have investigated the dependence of the efficiency of the LF EMF on seeds from Cosmo-geophysical parameters [30]. Primarily because, in recent years, the practice of agriculture of Kazakhstan has promoted a high-tech processing for pre-sown seed crops. Indeed, Professor A.M. Ashirov and his co-workers [29-30] assert any increase in qualitative and quantitative indicators (with a significant increase of plant immunity), thought to resist drought or the various agricultural diseases, is significantly accelerated - along with the maturation of crops.

The problem of solar-terrestrial relations, or, more accurately, a space-physics correlations with terrestrial processes, is increasingly attracting the attention of researchers from diverse specialties. There is even a visible alternative paradigm regarding this new knowledge. Certainly, the fluctuations of interplanetary magnetic fields seems disparagingly small when compared to the Earth's geomagnetic fields. All making it hard to believe that these weak electromagnetic disturbances may cause significant changes in climate, the biosphere, or the physiology of animals and plants, etc. Nevertheless, it is true.

Any object (animate or inanimate) can be represented as a "bundle of energy" or, more precisely, as energy information. Starting from the atom, all the way up to complex systems having their own character, an excellent memory, and the ability to exchange information with the surrounding environment. Postulated so, this exchange of information is carried out through cyclical regularities, which are best considered elementary transcendental functions: processes such as the sine wave, for instance, which has neither beginning nor end. Relatedly, our heart works within these modes of pulsation, as well as the growth of plants.

The essence of these fundamental discoveries - arising out of academician N.A. Kozyrev's work (referenced as "energy information exchanges in nature"), - has led us to the idea of consciously adjusting the physical and chemical processes in developing plants. After all, the notion of possibly changing plant genetics via the application of mathematical programming and synchronized exposure to the fluctuations of geomagnetic fields at a given point on our Earth is revolutionary. Indeed, time parameters, biorhythms and a frequency of intro-globular transformation through vibrations and energies lower than the energy of hydrogen bonds adapts the whole notion of agriculture.

In our search for the truth regarding the unity, integrity, and interconnectedness of all objects in our Universe, new patterns of amplification and the bio-resonant activation of crops, is established. The novelty of these relationships being confirmed by a patent of the Republic of Kazakhstan "A method for processing seeds and planting material» (№ 2002 / 05.04.1 / Ashirov A.M. Overall, these copyright certificates and diplomas of scientific discovery - issued by the International Association of Authors of Scientific Discoveries and Inventions (Moscow city), the International Academy of Authors of Scientific Discoveries "The pattern of bio-resonance activation of crops' seeds» (№ 272 / 14.12.2004 / Ashirov AM, with the staff) seize the future. Now, the "essence" of this pattern is as follows:

The previously unknown pattern of activation of bio-resonance amplification of seed crops and the fact that when electromagnetic seed is treated by a frequency which is a multiple of their biorhythms, during periods of

minimum values of gravitational forces, and the maximum intensity of cosmic radiation, a degree of bio-resonance activation of plant seeds is enhanced. All leading to an increase in the germination rate, yield and improved quality of productivity.

The main areas of application being: cotton, cereals (wheat, barley, rice, etc.).

This proposed technology provides a method to influence biorhythms in crop activity through natural and artificial electromagnetic fields. The central feature of this technology being to synchronize these effects with the fluctuations of the geomagnetic field (at a given point) of the earth – relative to the introduction of emissions from near and far space, as well as with their own biorhythms and frequencies at an intro-globular level of transformation.

For the first time, we have explained the systematic influence of bio-rhythms in plants, due to gravitational fields around the Sun, Moon, Earth and other planets: along with the electromagnetic fields generated by the Sun. Additionally, any artificial electromagnetic radiation with a frequency, which is a multiple of the biorhythms in plant seed's has been explored.

This impact on the metabolism of plant cells moves productivity to a higher energy level by increasing their biological activity. Every discovery reliably confirmed by an increase in the activity of alpha and beta-amylase, coupled with the hydrolysis of starch and dextrin endosperm to oligo-, di- and monosaccharaides consumed as food by seedlings and the roots of plants. Indeed, the embryo increases the synthesis of gibberellins, resulting in the accelerated development of root systems. Hence, a vigorous start during germination and the rapid transition to an autotrophic type of food is formed in plants by a strong photosynthetic apparatus.

CHAPTER VI

An Experimental Technique

1. Methods of calculating the seasonal-time schedules for the pre-plant treatment of seeds and planting material.

All things considered, the method of determining the correct timing for any pre-plant treatment of seeds and planting material, needs careful handling. So stated, let the centre of the Earth must be coordinated systematically (Figure 1). As such, the Earth and the Moon will align with a common centre of gravity (c.c.g.) due to the difference of the masses of these bodies. All resulting in the Earth's rotating around its axis and the rotation of the Moon around the Earth (c.c.g.) understood as a mobile system, wherein an interval [OA] describes a curve, where (.) A – c.c.g, [OA] < P, P – is Earth's radius. This c.c.g always belongs to the interval [s], with (.) B – as the centre of lunar activities. For example, suppose that at some time the Moon is in position 1, then c.c.g is located in 1 (.) After which (.) B moves to position 2, then c.c.g (.) A is in position 2, etc.

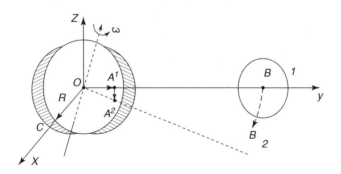

Figure 1

A similar - though less marked influence on the tides, is made by the Sun. Indeed, the forces of the Moon and Sun can be calculated as vectors, wherein the resultant changes in time - during the day, month, and year – become appreciable. Hence, the maximum tide corresponds to a position wherein the Sun, Earth and Moon line up - when the direction to the centre of the Earth from the Moon makes an angle of 90 ° (Figure 2). Studies finding that the most favourable conditions for the resonance observed (at minimum values) is during tidal turning. Therefore, it is necessary to calculate time in such a way that the position of 90 ° between the lines connecting the Earth and the Moon, or the Earth and the Sun, is on a perpendicular plane to the lines connecting the centre of the Earth with a point of latitude. In other words, where it is supposed pre-sowing planting materials will thrive.

In addition to the tidal forces acting on the Earth and global (non-tidal) gravitational forces, periodic disturbances need to be included in every calculation. This fact is reflected in the principle of parallelism. In future, therefore, additional allowances for earth's gravitational forces, the forces of the gravitational effects of the Sun and the Moon, the centrifugal force generated by the rotation of the earth on its axis, the centrifugal force produced by the rotation of the Earth around the Sun, the centrifugal force produced by the rotation of the Earth-Moon pair - all demand that adjustments to any calculation technique are meticulously honoured.

Moreover, some enhancement of this effect is clarified (strangely) by taking into account the position of the Moon in a specific zodiacal sign. Observably, the position of the Moon in some constellations favourably affects certain specific types of biological object. Each sign of the Zodiac being annually visited by the moon some 12-13 times! In these astral sectors, each zodiacal sign witnesses the Moon remaining about 2.5 days, i.e., during the year, our Moon is "in a sign" (e.g., Pisces).

Explicably, 2,5x12 = 30 days, because one can easily add one day "to" a certain zodiacal sign as well as one day "after", then adding another 2x12 = 24 days. Only 54 days! This is 1/7 of every day calculated in the year (54 days for each "star" of the 7). So, with the help of star charts (Figure 4) - and an applicator wheel to find out which stars and constellations will be above the horizon, where the company is supposed to be sowing and planting on the dates scheduled, one may proceed.

Now, Card and invoice terms, first of all, are necessarily pasted - or thick cardboard is used in the trim to make an inner circle notch on one of the closed lines with a certain latitude. Obviously, the latitude of the place in which a map is supposed to be used: for Shymkent, a latitude of 43 °, for Edinburgh (United Kingdom), a latitude of 56 °.

Moreover, any use of the map is as follows: a consignment circle is placed on the map to highlight the desired hour (hours marked on the edge of the star map). Then, in a "cut out" an overlay circle will be of those constellations and individual stars that are currently on the horizon, and it is in these directions and map positions relative to the horizon that work is undertaken. Obviously, the edge of the "cut out" in the trim circle marks the horizon, while near the centre of the cut is the zenith. Furthermore, the points of the horizon circle marked on the trim (according to card readings with the observed picture of the sky) will be full if the card is located above a horizontal: drawing the edge with the word "north" to the northern point of the horizon. If the card is on the table, we must remember that it reflects the position of the stars that are at the top and move them (mentally pictured) across the sky – respectively, horizon lines must be on the sides. Working with the card, one must also remember that the constellations are depicted with a few distorted and stretched forms, because the celestial sphere, as well as the globe, cannot be represented on a plane without distortion.

It goes without saying that the radial line on the map is a declination circle. The corresponding hours of Right Ascension being specified at the edge of the card. Additionally, for The Dec., bodies are concentric circles drawn every 30 ° (a third from the centre of the circle - the Celestial Equator - declination 0 °), (Figure 10). Hence, the eccentric circle on the map - the ecliptic, is the point of intersection with the celestial equator at a right ascension, is congruent with signs of (the vernal equinox) and the 12 g (autumnal equinox) (Figure 10).

It is useful to note the position of the Sun at the ecliptic, while a star map will allow even greater observational convenience. Any computer processing of data on the effects of near and far space, the characteristics of the Earth's geomagnetic field, Moon phases in signs of the Zodiac, as well as the determine of grain biorhythms periods in pre-plant treatment, is equally helpful.

The processing time for seeds of a specific family should be in indicated by straight lines plotted on the basis of the "parallel lines" principle – each established empirically:

$$X_1 = (Y-b_1)\backslash a_1,$$
$$X_2 = (Y - b_2)\backslash a_2,$$
$$X_n = (Y-b_n)\backslash a_n$$

where – y corresponding to the day, and $y>b_1$ $y>b_2$,.... $y>b_n$.

Thus, for example, for Merke (Jambul) in 1999, the rime was identified (by local time) 15.09.1999,.: 0^{00}, 5^{00}, 7^{00}, 9^{00}, 12^{00}, 13^{00}, 16^{00}, 19^{00}, 20^{00}, 22^{00}.

For Ostrogorki Sandyktau district of the Akmola region in 2000, 9 May: 2^{00}-7^{00},11^{00}-13^{00},17^{00}-18^{00}.

For the Zhalagash district of Kyzylorda region, in 2001, May 11th, one may observe: 1^{00}, 3^{00}, 6^{00}, 11^{00}, 16^{00}. The point at which these lines are built being prepared with the help of computer data. Indeed, the programme takes into account all these factors. Compiled calculation algorithms and adverse blago¬priyatnyh days for pre-treatment (specifically for this area) taking into account the fact that plants, like all biological objects are not a closed system. Especially so, when calculating cosmic gravitational resonance and the relationship between the Sun, Earth, Moon and planets of our solar system.

Interestingly, the gravitational force acting on each material particle on the Earth's surface is the result of two major components: the force of gravity, directed towards the center of the earth and the centrifugal force perpendicular to the axis of rotation of the Earth. Our Earth, of course, as a cosmic body is part of the gravity of the Sun - Earth - Moon. For one synodic Moon cycle simultaneously two harmonic vibrations with the same frequency in mutually perpendicular directions may be detected. There are many pendulums - "Earth and the planets of the solar system" concerning the common center of gravity - the Sun, and the place of their "attachment" in the Universe - the core of the Galaxy. Then the Sun - the star of the Galaxy, has a pendulum around its center - the nucleus of the Galaxy, etc. Our work takes into account the gravitational influence of the Earth, which manifests itself in tidal power. These tidal forces add vectors, while the resultant changes in time during the day, month, year are significant. All calculations being taken from the Institute of Theoretical Astronomy of Standard Programmes Barycentric Coordinates, the Institute of Geodesy and Cartography and Krasovsky, NASA data along with the Internet.

Subsequent calculations of daily fluctuations in accordance with Newton's third law, we performed on a personal computer. In addition, regarding the preparation of schedules for pre-plant treatment et al, we used the data analysis of the relationship of oscillations in solar activity and the geomagnetic field of the Earth. (Novosibirsk-99, e-mail hasnulin@ngs.ru.)

Thus, the explanation for the mechanism of effect, low frequency, EMF must result in a comprehensive study of the biological, physical and chemical-quantum-cal features of an object, as well as the rhythmic patterns of influence of the external factors on those biological rhythms that reflect the various manifestations of solar and geomagnetic activity, tidal variations of "gravity" , Wolf numbers (W), solar radio flux density, the intensity of the neutron component of cosmic rays, normalized atmospheric pressure (CL), the daily index of geomagnetic activity (Kc), a planetary index of geomagnetic activity (Ap), the critical frequency of ionospheric layers (F2), the speed movement of the geocentric orbit of the Moon (V), the means of daily tidal variations of gravity (G) etc, to coordinate Almaty, Kostanay, Petropavlovsk, Kyzylorda and other locations.

Any calculation of daily options regarding the position of the Moon for a particular area (length L, the phase angle FA, declination, latitude, elevation angle, the climax), being made by a doctor. Phys. mat. Sciences, Professor V.G. Teyfel.

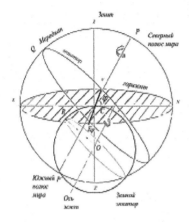

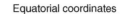
Equatorial coordinates

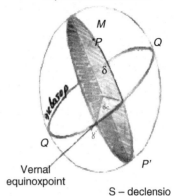

Vernal equinoxpoint

S – declensio

L – direct ascensionn

$\varphi = \angle COR$ – Geographica latitudeof the place;

$h = \angle PCN$ – The height of the pole above the horizon;

$h = 90° - \varphi + S$ (1)

The equation (1) shows the relationship between the height (h) of lights (M) in the upper culmination, its declination (S) and

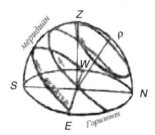

Daily path of light on the horizon for an observer located in the middle latitudes.

Direct ascension is usually expressed in units of time. For example:

15° – 1 hour, 1o – 4 minutes,
15' – 1 minute, 15" - 1 second.
7h 18 min = 109" 30'

Indexes G, K_L, A_R recorded observatories (such as Novosibirsk), the index of f_0 F_2 -ionospheric station Tomsk.

The mathematical apparatus rather complicated and is given in an abbreviated form.

1. The basic equation for calculating the parameters cosmogeophysical

1.1 *General view*

Under tide-acceleration $\vec{a}$ we understand the difference between the absolute acceleration produced outside the body (the Moon, Sun, planets, and others.) on the surface and in the centre of the Earth. Let:

$\vec{r} = r\vec{R}$ - geocentric radius vector of the external attracting body, it is the radius vector from the centre of the Earth's centre of mass of the outer body;

$\vec{\rho} = \rho\vec{P}$ - geocentric radius of the point on the surface of Earth (geocentric radius vector of topocentre);

$\vec{d} = d\vec{D}$ - topocentric radius vector of the external body;

$\vec{R}, \vec{P}, \vec{D}$ - the corresponding unit vector.

In this notation, the basic equation is:

$$\vec{a} = \frac{\mu}{d^2}\vec{D} - \frac{\mu}{r^2}\vec{R}, \tag{1}$$

where

$$\vec{d} = \vec{r} - \vec{\rho}, d^2 = r^2 + \rho^2 - 2r\rho(\vec{R}\vec{P}), \vec{D} = [\vec{r} - \vec{\rho}]/d \tag{2}$$

Parentheses (.) denotes the scalar product of vectors:

$$\vec{R}, \vec{P} = R_x P_x + R_y P_y + R_z P_z$$

$\mu=Gm$ - gravitational parameter of the external body, G - the gravitational constant, m - mass of the outer body.

1.2 *Linearization.*

Substituting (2) into (1) expanding the resulting expression in powers of the small parameter $\varepsilon = \rho/r$ and retaining only the first-order terms, thereby obtaining the linearized basic equation:

$$\vec{a} = \frac{\mu\varepsilon}{r^2}\left[3(\vec{R}\vec{P})\vec{R} - \vec{P}\right] \tag{3}$$

Casting off the remaining term of the last formula is

$$\vec{\Delta} = \frac{\mu\varepsilon^2}{r^2}\left[-\frac{3}{2}\vec{R} + \frac{15}{2}(\vec{R}\vec{P})^2\vec{R} - 3(\vec{R}\vec{P})\vec{P}\right] + (\text{Parts from } 3) + \ldots \tag{4}$$

It can be shown that the linear model (3) maximum relative error Δ/a is still 1.5ε, and this value is achieved when the vectors $\vec{R}, \vec{P}$ are collinear (parallel or antiparallel) or orthogonal. For the closest major celestial body - the Moon - the value of ε is approximately equal to $1/60$. Consequently, the relative Moon error does not exceed 2.5%. For other bodies in the solar system (the Sun, planets, etc.) it is generally negligible.

1.3 *Qualitative analysis of equation (3).*

Accelerations from one external body attaching both a symmetrical line connecting the centre of the earth and the centre of the outer body (rotational symmetry), and one relative to a plane passing through the centre of the earth orthogonally to the line (mirror symmetry). Distortion symmetries induced discarded the remainder (4). However, small links and can be ignored (for the Moon they are no more than 1 degree in angle and, as already mentioned, not more than 2.5% in magnitude).

On the Earth's surface, calculations are divided into four specific sets of points. The first set consists of only two points nearest to the outer body - and the most distant from it ("tidal pole"). In these vectors $\vec{r}, \vec{\rho}$ are collinear points. Acceleration is directed outwards from the centre of the earth and takes a maximum value $2\mu\varepsilon/r^2$, and the tangential component is equal to zero.

The second set - points on a circle, separated from the tidal pole 90 degrees (point "tidal equator"). This tide-acceleration is directed into the earth and has a minimum value of $\mu\varepsilon/r^2$, tangential compiling also zero.

The third set - a point separated from the tidal equator of about 35 degrees to either side. Here, the normal component is zero.

Finally, the fourth set - a point lying midway between the equator and the poles (they are separated by 45 degrees). Here, the tangential component takes its maximum value $3\mu\varepsilon/(2r^2)$.

1.4 *Some numerical estimates.*

Below are the values of the tide creating acceleration in "tidal poles" for the various bodies of the solar system in order of magnitude. The values are given in mkgl (1 mkgl = 10^{-6} cm/s^2). Furthermore, the land is considered to be a ball with a radius of 6371.024 km.

Moon at a minimum distance (perigee)	130.3 mkgl
Moon average distance	110.0 mkgl
Moon at the maximum distance (apogee)	93.7 mkgl
Sun at the minimum distance (perihelion)	53.1 mkgl
Sun at an average distance of	50.5 mkgl
Sun at maximum distance (aphelion)	48.0 mkgl
Venus at a minimum distance of	5.8 * 10-3 mkgl
Jupiter is at a minimum distance of	6.5 * 10-4 mkgl
Mars is at a minimum distance of	1.1 * 10-4 mkgl
Mercury at a minimum distance of	3.6 * 10-5 mkgl
Saturn is at a minimum distance of	$2.3*10^{-5}$ mkgl

(Note. The data obtained by the Moon on the basis of a simplified model of a Keplerian orbit, the actual scope of the minimum to the maximum value is greater than the table shows. We also note that if you change the height of 1-meter acceleration due to gravity near the surface of the Earth, it changes to 308 mkgl).

As is evident from these estimates, the main effect is given to the Moon and Sun, so the equation with regard to their joint effect is written as:

$$\vec{a} = \frac{\mu_m \rho}{r_m^3}\left[3(\vec{R}_m\vec{P})\vec{R}_m - \vec{P}\right] + \frac{\mu_s \rho}{r_s^3}\left[3(\vec{R}_s\vec{P})\vec{R}_s - \vec{P}\right] \qquad (5)$$

Where μ_m, r_m, R_m - parameters related to the Moon, μ_s, r_s, R_s - parameters related to the Sun, and ρ = 6371.024 km - the average radius of the Earth, that is the radius of the sphere whose volume is equal to the volume of the Earth ellipsoid.

1.5 *The working version of the basic equation.*

Gravitational parameters of the Moon and Sun, and the average radius of the Earth are the result of calculations - not directly from observations. To reduce the number of unobservable parameters transforming the equation (5), we estimate as follows. Multiply, and divide it by a free fall acceleration $g = \mu\varepsilon/\rho^2$ = 982.024 gl = 9.82024*10^8 mkgl.

(μ_e = 398603*10^9 m^3/s^2 – Regarding Earth's gravitational parameter), we note that the mass ratio of the Moon and Earth is 1 / 81.30 while the ratio of the mass of the Sun and Earth is equal to 332,951 – and when normalizing the equatorial radius of the Earth R_0 = 6378.160 km (rather than a mean radius ρ = 6371.024 km). Then we get in units mkgl:

$$\vec{a} = 9.787*0^8\left\{\frac{1}{8.9}\left(\frac{R_0}{r_m}\right)^3\left[3(\vec{R}_m\vec{P})\vec{R}_m - \vec{P}\right] + 332951\left(\frac{R_0}{r_s}\right)^3\left[3(\vec{R}_s\vec{P})\vec{R}_s - \vec{P}\right]\right\} \qquad (6)$$

The brace is a dimensionless vector-quantity of the order of 10^{-7} on the module - the first term refers to the Moon, the second - to the Sun.

1.6 *Some remarks.*

1. Formally, the equation (6) contains 8 parameters: two parameters - the geographic coordinates of ϕ, λ, three parameters - the coordinates of

the Moon and another three parameters - the coordinates of the Sun. However, since the position of the Moon and Sun are functions of time, in fact, the tide-acceleration depends on three variables: ϕ, λ, time.

2. We can offer two methods for calculating the acceleration of tides:

    a. Use well-known expansions of spherical (trigonometric) functions. In this case, the theory of motion regarding the Moon and Sun are included explicitly in terms of coefficients of these expansions and through trigonometric arguments;

    b. A direct calculation of the coordinates of external bodies and the subsequent application of the formula (6). Hereafter, we shall always keep in mind this is the second method.

3. All the above applies to a point on the Earth's surface. If necessary, the calculations for the geographical coordinates (ϕ, λ), which are under the Earth's surface at a depth h km, can be undertaken in the following manner: Run by the formula (6) the calculation of the surface of the Earth with the same (ϕ, λ) and multiply the result by a factor of k = 1 - h/6371.024. This follows from the fact that the expression (5) is linearly dependent on ρ.

f = 1.95 Cal/(cm^2× min) = 1.36 × 10^6 erg/(cm^2× s) » 1370 W/m^2.

Variability within a cycle of about 0.1%.

Total solar radiation:

$L_\odot$= 3.826 · 1033 erg / sec

The radiation flux from the surface of the Sun:

F = 6.284 · 1010 erg / (cm^2· s)

Understanding this picture depends on EMF effects in biological systems and their sensitivity to fluctuations in the geomagnetic and cosmo-physical flows. Each allowing interpretations of both the stimulating and inhibitory effects of EMF. Compatibility analysis graphs and time-equation yields for plots regarding their temporal processing and intra-day charts, along with biorhythm charts, allows adjustments to any subsequent year.

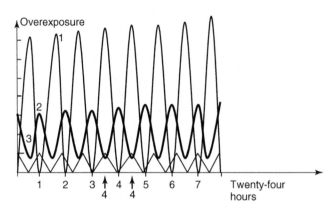

Figure 3. Week cycles helio insolation - (1.7 cycles), Lunar attraction - 2 (7.8 cycles) and M-radiation regions of the Sun - 3 (7.9 cycles), the optimal time of artificial exposure - 4-4 *

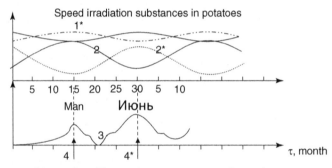

Figure 4. Monthly cycle of lunar gravity, corpuscular radiation m-regions of the Sun and the level of their own metabolism potatoes and time of artificial exposure

For scheduling or developing methods of preparing planting material and the processing of low-frequency electromagnetic fields, we have developed a special programme - MONOGRAF. As such, fundamental aspects of the programme may be listed in the public domain. Firstly, the Moon moves around the Earth in an elliptical orbit, obviously, so the distance from the Earth to the Moon varies from a minimum of 356 400 km perigee to a

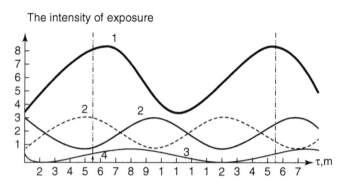

Figure 5. Annual dependinghelio insolation (1), the lunar attraction (2 - 2 *) Natural (3) and artificial electromagnetic (4) Radiation

maximum apogee of 406,700 km. Accordingly, the changes and degree of tidal influence on our globe depending on the position of the Moon relative to the Sun (because the Sun also has a tidal effect on the Earth) fluctuate due to the various distances of these bodies. Tidal effects, therefore, are manifested in the fact that the diameter of the Earth - equal to 12 756 km (about one-thirtieth of the distance to the Moon) and the lunar gravity force acting on our globes face, is much larger than the current in the opposite side of it. All meaning, the difference of forces causes a slight deformation of the Earth's crust, along with a large tidal wave in the oceans and in the atmosphere. So claimed, the effect of these solar tides becomes smaller as the diameter of the Earth compared to the distance from the Sun (149.5 million km) descends into the negligible. The position of the Moon in orbit (Fig. 1) is defined by longitude 1, counted from the moment of a New Moon (N) or phase angle (PA), which is equal to 180 degrees in the New Moon, and 0 (360) degrees regarding a Full Moon (R). Measured, of course, by a Full Moon when viewed clockwise.

Tidal effects in specific places across the world also depends on the Moons declination δ and latitude ϕ (Fig. 6), since these values are determined by maximum angular height above the horizon - where the Moon reaches its climax.

Obviously, along with the maximum declination of the Moon, the greatest positive effects should occur in the northern hemisphere: with a negative decline in the south. Thusly, research into any (possible) impact through the position of the Moon, or that of the processes in our world, must take into accounts all of these factors.

MOONGRAF programmes provides two files to access and coordinate the position of the Moon on each date of a given month. This programme is suitable for non-astronomical studies involving any comparison of experimental data for various biological processes - with the position and movement of the Moon.

Since the greatest effect regarding a possible impact of the Moon on our Earth is processed at a given point, we can expect to see the maximum height of the Moon above the horizon. All the data tables are attached to the climax of the Moon: that is, calculated precisely for this moment.

A table given for each day shows the following values: the date, the decline of the moon - the angular distance of the Moon from the equator to the north (positive declination), or south (negative declination). Also, the *celestial equator* - the intersection of the plane of Earth's equator with

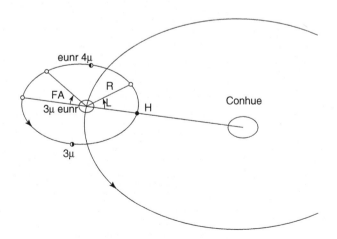

Figure 6.

the celestial sphere conditional. The **climax of the Moon** - the time of the passage of the moon over a point on the south maternity (Kazakhstan winter) and the time/point of observation. The **phase** angle - the angle measured from the point of a Full Moon in a clockwise direction from 0 to 360 degrees. The **distance** - geocentric distance to the Moon in kilometers; the angular height - the **angular height** of the Moon above the horizon at the moment of climax (the south point); the **age of the moon**, measured in days from the time of a New Moon. The **Zodiac sign** in which the Moon is present.

Table 1 The relative values of distances and angles on the height of the Moon
The horizon for the city of Almaty in January 2009

Day	The phase angle (degrees)	The illuminated part lunar disk	The distance of the Moon from Earth (km)	Declension Moon (degrees)	Time coolies Nation (h, m)	The angular height of the Moon in the nation-Kulm (degrees)	Sign Zodiac
1	2	3	4	5	6	7	8
2	-131	0,17	395106	-7,3	16,32	40	Pisces
3	-119	0,25	390532	-1,6	17,13	45	Pisces
4	-108	0,35	385236	4,2	17,56	51	Pisces
5	-96	0,45	379507	9.9	18,42	57	Aries
6	-84	0,56	373733	15,4	19,29	62	Aries
7	-71	0,66	367113	20.7	20,28	68	Taurus
8	-58	0.77	362826	24.3	21,23	71	Taurus
9	-44	0,86	361947	26,0	21,53	73	Gemini
10	-30	0,9	359819	26,9	22,56	74	Gemini
11	-1	0,98	358350	25,9	00,02	73	Cancer

Day	The phase angle (degrees)	The illu-minated part lunar disk	The dis-tance of the Moon from Earth (km)	Declen-sion Moon (degrees)	Time coolies Nation (h, m)	The angular height of the Moon in the nation-Kulm (degrees)	Sign Zodiac
12	-2	1,00	35857	23,0	01,05	70	Cancer
13	12	0,99	361181	18,0	02,09	65	Leo
14	26	0,95	365023	12,	03,01	59	Leo
15	39	0,89	370110	5,4	03,59	52	Virgo
16	53	0,80	376061	-0,8	04,44	46	Virgo
17	65	0,71	382408	-6,9	05,28	40	Libra
18	77	0,61	388645	-12,4	06,11	34	Libra
19	89	0,51	394299	-17,2	06,54	30	Libra
20	100	0,41	398987	-21,6	07,46	25	Scorpio
21	111	0,32	402477	-2405	08,31	22	Scorpio
22	122	0,23	404696	-26,3	09,17	20	Sagittarius
23	133	0,16	405729	-26,6	09,37	20	Sagittarius
24	144	0,09	405762	-26,9	10,26	20	Sagittarius
25	155	0,05	404729	-25,3	11,23	21	Capricorn
26	166	0,02	403285	-22,8	12,11	24	Capricorn
27	177	0,00	401417	-19,3	12,57	28	Aquarius
28	-172	0,01	399165	-14,9	13,41	32	Aquarius
29	-160	0,03	396504	-9,9	14,24	37	Aquarius
30	-149	0,07	392521	-2,9	15,16	44	Pisces
31	-137	0,13	388780	2,8	16,00	50	Pisces
32	-125	0,21	384588	8,6	16,44	55	Aries

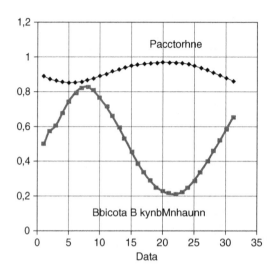

Figure 8

Thus, according to the value of the magnitude of decline, the distance of the Moon from the Earth and other tabular data from 05.01.09 on 11.01.09 tidal forces of the Moon are minimal, with 17.01.09 on 23.01.09 maximized. A comparison of these values is best if tracked by a chart (Figure 8), which is based on table data using the Excel spreadsheet. According to this schedule, therefore, one can judge the time when the greatest, or least, effect of the tidal influence for a given observation point occurs. In the northern hemisphere the greatest impact falls on a match (or proximity) - a minimum distance of the moon with a maximum height above the horizon in the climax - with a positive declination of the Moon. This programme was tested and showed good results on examples of pre-plant treatment for planting materials. In this paper, therefore, we investigate the effect of low-frequency dependence of the efficiency of the electromagnetic field regarding seeds and the tidal effects of the Moon.

The height of the Moon (red line) above the horizon for Almaty city in January 2009

The above estimates for effective seed treatment based on the value of the tidal forces of the Moon agree with our previously published work [17-19].

Indeed, MOONGRAF calculated the optimum time for a pre-treatment of seeds. As such, a pre-sowing treatment by low-frequency electromagnetic fields on seeds is one way to improve the qualities of crops: thereby increasing yields. The main advantage of this technology is its ability to improve growth and development through the mobilization of internal reserves within the seeds themselves - without chemical treatment. Also, the advantages of this treatment are cost-effectiveness and simplicity. For example, field tests have shown that the plants grown from treated seeds - through low-frequency electromagnetic fields (EMF LF) have many advantages. Especially when compared to other systems. Indeed, they had a strong root system (figure 5-6-7-8) superior control adjustment, vegetative mass, stem thickness, the number of leaves on the stem, the size and number of cobs etc. All proving to be more resistant to drought, diseases and pests - finally surpassing the control of the yield to 51.3% (Fig. 3).

Thus, this programme allows one to calculate the relative importance of the tidal effects anywhere on Earth. For instance, knowing the coordinates of any point in South America will make it possible to determine the date of minimum, or maximum, tidal effects. It should be noted, of course, that the mechanism of the effect of lunar tides on biological processes in plants and animals is not exactly known. Requiring, as it does, specially designed and long-term experiments to safely install, as well as explain, the relationship of biochemical processes to phenomena with different kinds of cosmic factors, which include the tidal effects of the Moon.

2. Treatment methods of seeds and field experience

The processing of seed

The vehicle with the best technological equipment and specialities fitted directly to the point of storage for seeds goes straight into the interior of a warehouse.

1. The operator shall make the equipment for the vehicle. The modulator must be stored in its case. The two outputs of the modulator are

connected to the positive and negative poles of this "cars" battery (red output being connected to plus) and a switch modulator transferred to the position of "network".

2. After warming the modulator for 3 minutes, its slot is connected with 2 antennas: each antenna being cord length - 10 meters. Hence, antennas are placed "cross form" and the seed must be between the antennas. Certainly, antennas have to lie down directly on the seeds, while the distance between the antennas should not exceed 10 meters.

The circuit arrangement of instrumental resources

1. The presence of flashing on the display modulator and antenna after connection, talking about the beginning of the treatment process, i.e., emission of electromagnetic waves, links to the start and end of a fixed treatment.

2. The inoculum may be in any container and any quantity may be "etched" as repackaging is not required.

3. If the seed load and the area occupied by it is huge, then processing is produced by a greater amount of machines, until the treatment of the entire volume of seeds is achieved.

4. The processing time (exposure) of seeds must be calculated in advance - and issued to operators in the form of graphs. The operators must strictly adhere to these schedules in operation.

5. In order to avoid the impact of the modulator on control seeds, treatment is prohibited on these seeds (directly) in the field during sowing. The control box should be the place of treatment at a distance of 1.5-2 km.

6. Upon completion of processing, the modulator is switched off transfer switch from a position of "network" and disconnected from the battery. Antennas are pulled out from the socket and gently fold modulator. All technical equipment is transferred to the car.

7. After completion of the processing of seeds to make notes in a special statement, where the seating area, the area name of economy, team, date and time (start and end) processing, seed variety, its quantity. The

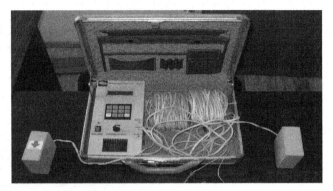

Figure 9. The modulator NEMI-15

signatures of the chief agronomist brigade foreman and An operator shall certify entries in the journal.

8. After 10 days the link again come to this farm repeats the processing of the above scheme, the remaining seeds. Moreover, so every 10 days is the seed treatment before their full seeding.

Arrangement of instrument and other means:

Features the pre-plant treatment of seeds, or planting material, in the electromagnetic field as described below.

This proposed technology can be widely used in agriculture in order to obtain higher yields and improved quality through a pre-plant treatment of seeds EMM.

Any strong development of seedlings provides active plant photosynthesis, which increases by 1.5 times. Such plants better absorb minerals and nitrogen fertilizers, thereby giving (eventually) not only higher yields, but also an improvement in the quality of produce. For example, an increase in the amount of proteins and gluten in cereal, as well as legume crops, not to mention the amount of oleic acid in oilseed crops has been noted. Furthermore, as a result of exposure to electromagnetic modulator stimulation, the immune system of plants, which makes them more resistant to diseases and

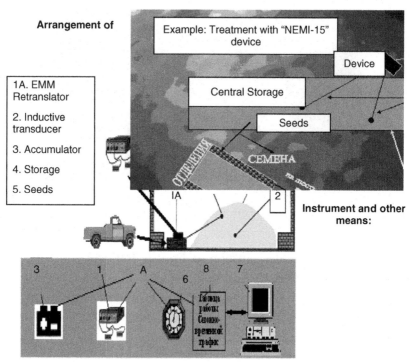

Figure 10. Stages of pre-sowing treatment

pests, actually allows these plants to develop an extra tolerance to adverse climatic conditions: drought, winds, temperature, etc. In experiments on small plots, or industrial areas with the same agricultural background and culture, "in cross" (in different climatic regions) produced positive results in all cases. An increased seed germination of 2-3 percent, shoots appeared 3-5 days early, while the speedy maturation of all crops occurred 7-14 days faster than in the control crops. The difference between the control and experimental harvest times for these crops was particularly impressive in the event of adverse weather conditions (drought, winds, temperature, etc.) - up to 20 to 30 percent better survival, or more. Hence, the proposed technology for our pre-sowing treatment is proving extremely simple and does not require tangible energy costs, or for that matter manual labour. A power

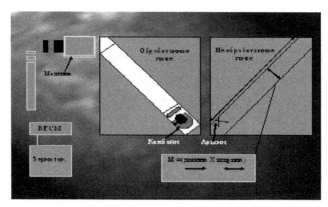

Figure 11. Scheme of control seed thrashing

modulator made from a car battery can operate on a direct current voltage of 12 volts. The inoculum may be in any container and any number of them may be etched, as repacking is required. Regarding time seed treatments - 11 minutes only is necessary. Also, the material should be sown within 10 days from the date of treatment, since the (10 day) stimulating effect on the treated seeds is markedly reduced. Thus, according to the Department of Agriculture of the Amur region, a significant difference from the control plants compared to treated plants was noticed -especially in the amount of buckwheat flower brushes obtained from seeds sown in the first week after treatment (within 10 days) – calculated at 24%, whereas those sown in the second week (9 -10 hours) - only 5%.

Thus, the economy, using applied technology, will not accrue additional energy costs or manual labour services through processing these products. Interestingly, the uniqueness of this technology lies in the fact that previous agricultural machinery has remained unchanged for so long. Indeed, experiments carried out on a number of soils (in reclamation and climatic zones) showed that this new technology only gave POSITIVE RESULTS. Moreover, there was an increase in proteins and gluten, not to mention oil yield with high levels of oleic acid, etc. Each being resistant to mutation and genetic modifications: including loci encoding biosynthesis gliadin gluteins, alpha- and beta-amylases, all of which are the most important and distinctive feature of our technology. As such, it was equally noted that an increase in the resistance of plants to diseases clearly indicated the activation of their immune systems. This property beingparticularly marked in animals fed on these products and confirmed in a document issued by the State Farm "Turkestanets" wherein EMM was used from November 1992 to February 1993 - the pig-breeding complex.

Bookmarking the experimental and control fields

To examine procedures comparatively (regarding an agronomic and economic evaluation of these technologies), it will be necessary to put in each farm, without exception, both experimental and control fields. Therein, experimental fields should be sown with treated seeds, while control fields with untreated materials. Manifestly, special attention must be paid to:

- The selection and preparation of the land for field tests and control;
- Size and re-plots;
- Placement of plots;
- Share experiences and techniques of control;
- Requirements of the agro-technical conditions for the laying of the plots;
- The selection and preparation of land for field experience and control.

Selecting a field for a bookmark "Experience/Control" is made on-site for (yield) fields. Unarguably, the chief agronomist determines the average site class, ie, the average yield between the best and worst of the yield fields. Moreover, in determining a fields "experience" it is important that – "monitoring" is always used to secure uniformity in agricultural backgrounds. Indeed, "experienced" and control crops should be on the same card whereon an agronomic background is more or less homogeneous. Therefore, to address the question of land suitability (withdrawn under the "experience") each element of prior economic history needs to be considered. Indeed, one must be completely clear regarding "experience" and control stations – particularly if a previous history is unknown. Overall, one must make sure that during the last 3 years of "experience" every crop year produced a culture wherein an applied uniform system for processing and fertilizers was documented.

Any land previously exposed to a different economic use (e.g., a past site afterwards made more fertile - such as a road, or garden, or corrals, etc.), can exhibit drastically different levels of soil fertility. A situation exactly the same, of course in the case of control or experimental areas without proper preparation. All making caution a vital component of practical application.

Thus, those lands reserved for the "experience" of renewed fertility should be uniform. Equal, in other words, for relief across their entirety. So, for its plot size (as a rule), it should be such that it could apply modern mechanization for cultivation and harvesting. Certainly, one must strive to properly accommodate all these options and control the "experience" of different soils, or ones with close differences.

The surface of the test and control areas must be extremely well planned. Unplanned production "experience" and control needs to be assiduously avoided. The question, therefore, of choosing cards for sowing should be resolved in advance of planting. These issues being addressed jointly with the heads of households or firms. All the discussill aspects of site selection, in the annex to the contract or in the contract written card number, which will be incorporated "experience" and controls.

Accommodation plots

These plots are located along the long side of their slope. This is due to the location of the plots (in a majority of cases), as well as the changes in soil fertility, i.e., each of the plots will be more or less equally covered by different grades of soil over the pilot area.

Equipment Share experiences

The placement of plots and their frequency, according to advances made by our calculated schematic plan, must be appropriate to the size of the parties in question.

As such, these schematic plans are made together with the heads of households, or firms, in order to start sowing companies. A copy of the plan card nonetheless being removed from any routing economy, although their application in terms of plot size is essential.

The layout of the plots and their repetition in the same field. Questions about ripening seeds

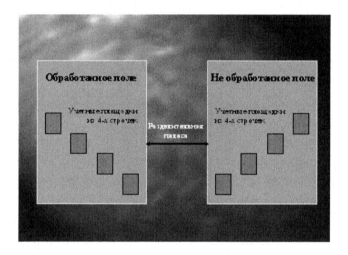

The economy of Central Asia, as a rule, holds that spring planting should be completed by late October. Some full-length grain is used as a seed selection for future planting companies (in May next year, i.e. 6-7 months). However, practice shows that grain before sowing should "ripen." In fact, ripening seeds require a 12 month "rest period" (for cotton) - atop the usually specified period. The spread of ripening, of course, depends on the energy-characteristics of the variety involved. Also, the environmental and agronomic conditions of plant growth, the timing and method of data collection and the storage conditions of these seeds are influential. Now, most farms have to sow seeds on immature fields. Hence, when sowing the obtained seeds, these factors can be overvalued by a 20-80% per consumption of seed grain, which in turn affects the economy as a whole.

Curiously, the phases of plant development are simultaneous, although, immature seeds long laid in the ground often die. Nevertheless, the process of ripening for these seeds is considered complete when the determination of germination accords with the vigour index. Overall, a retention period being necessary for improved maturity, vigour and seed germination. The efficacy of storage for the materials depending, of course, on the physiological state of the seeds (humidity, maturity, etc), as well as storage conditions themselves (the temperature and humidity of an environment).

Technology provides EMF exposure of the seed during storage; our treatment accelerating the ripening seeds progress, while increasing their germination and field germination.

Work should be carried out in three stages.

1. During the period of storage for the seeds (November-December).
2. After etching in the early spring (March-April).
3. Just before sowing.

The uniqueness of this technology lies in the fact that these low cost and rapid processes allow an acceleration of ripening and, almost, guaranteeing highly productive plants.

Our working experience in these areas (conducted in the Akmola region of Kazakhstan), clearly showed that seeds obtained from already treated plants were more susceptible to the energy-information effects of EMF. For instance, in the fields of LLP "Garysh" Esil district in 2005, there was a fixed yield in the control fields – 12 hwt \ ha, and for "experienced" materials 17,2 hwt \ ha. The yield increase was 17.2 - 12 = 5.2 hwt \ ha, and in 2006 re-EM seed treatment led to a yield increase of 6,0 hwt \ ha, which is 43 and 50%, respectively.

The implementation of phenological observations and accounting for experimental and control fields
Ongoing phenological observations and surveys on a variety of experimental and control plots should characterize the extent to which any implemented

technology contributes to early maturation and higher yields of wheat. As such, the authors conducted observations in all phases of the embryonic development of the shoot, booting, heading, flowering, and ripening. Furthermore, these observations were verified by highly qualified specialists on the scientific staff of leading scientific institutions in our republic: working under contract.

It should be noted that deeper steps into careful experimentation have been done in previous years, even though these observation and surveys were carried out under a simplified scheme.

Argued so, methods of observation and accounting are based on a technique SYUZNIHI as well as "Techniques of field experience" B.A.Dospehova. Therefore, debatably, this is the most appropriate procedure in any production environment. Moreover, accounting and monitoring needs to be undertaken at the borders of these two fields, whereon the dividing line in agricultural backgrounds comes as close together as possible. Indeed, this moment is the most important programme in accounting and supervision.

Thusly, any projected phenological observation and survey can be divided into six main phases:

1. The accounted seedling;
2. Accounting tillering, stem height measurements, etc.
3. The observations of the accounting rate "booting" heading and flowering;
4. Accounting maturing and fruiting;
5. The preparation of acts of approbation on certain biological yields.
6. The completion of these works.

After complete sowing has been made a "Certificate of Completion for the Treatment of Seed," can be issued - which is determined by the amount of treated seeds and sowing areas in hectares (form №1).

When the seedlings are seen in a field, the "experience/control" components of the "germination Act" may be finalized (Form №2).

Later, during the phenological observations by employees of the company, operatives may go into the fields 1-2 times (if necessary), each visit being entered in a field book about the development and tillering of plant. A document eventually signed by the decision makers of both parties. When ripe, harvest workers can leave the field for a compilation of the "Act of testing the Harvest" (form number 3), which is determined by biological productivity. Afterwards, at the end of the harvesting, this campaign can be summarised and filed with a "Certificate of Verification of the Executed Works and Settlement" (form number 4).

CHAPTER **VII**

Appropriating and Implementing Innovative Technologies

The technology aforementioned has been successfully tested in all regions subordinated to the Ministry of Agriculture, including research institutes and "experienced stations." Particularly of note in this regard is the Research Institute named after Barayev, Kotanay in North Kazakhstan. Never forgetting, of course, the Aral Sea regions Rice Research Institute, the South Kazakhstan Research Institute, as well as the foreign-stock "Elite Seeds of Tatarstan" in Kazan. Also, the Chelyabinsk Research Institute, the Deutshe-Russisches Instityt fur Biomagnettische Kybernetik und Nanoteshnologie, Berlin, the Agro university named after Suleiman Dimerel of Sparta, Turkey, the Research Institutes of Ukraine, Uzbekistan, and Tajikistan all played necessary parts. Tellingly, the technology was tested in 6 regions of Kazakhstan and 8 states: each recording very positive results. Indeed, the increase in yield was - 30-40%. Furthermore, the results for 11 crops, including wheat, barley, rice, corn, potatoes, and others, were significantly above expectation. All testifying to the universality, sustainability and adaptability of this technology. In Kazakhstan, which has a 12.65 million Ha acreage, any grain, yield increase will (potentially) be 5-6 million. These tons clearly contributing to the food security of our country. According to conservative estimates, therefore, ($ 200 per ton of wheat) will be equivalent to 1.0-1.2 billion US dollars. Overall, the economic effect (net of expenses), being 0.9-1.0 billion in US dollars per year. All factors published in "Kazakhstanskaya Pravda" newspaper on 30.04.2005. Additionally, "A discovery of global significance", Megapolis newspaper № 9 (222) 05.03.2005", "In the glory",

18.04.2005, "A revolutionary breakthrough" magazine "AgroƏlem" 01(06)2010 p.24, "Electromagnetic fields of fertility," as well as the television programme "Kazakh TV» of 24.11.2014, Kazakhstanskaya Pravda. № 95 (27716) 16.05.2014, "A scientist of the SKR edges towards a Nobel Prize" 18.04.2014 Agroinfo. № 12 (96) of 07.14.2014, "A Kazakhstan scientist claims the Nobel Prize" Egemen Kazakhstan newspaper, "I wish that kazakh people would benefit first from my scientific work" 06/08/2014, freedom of speech, "Project 272: feed the world" 06/05/2014 g, Southern Kazakhstan, № 56 (19385) 05.21.2014, the "Long Road to Nobel" - are sources worthy of exploration.

The marketing conducted so far has shown that this technology can have a stabilizing effect overall, since it allows agricultural work on restricted areas. Moreover, in the climatically diverse regions of Russia, Ukraine, Kazakhstan, Uzbekistan, Tajikistan, Germany and Turkey, positive results were obtained. Indeed, the germination of seeds for 3-5 days and their early maturation by 7-10 days, was regularized. Equally, the differences between the control and experimental harvest crops being 30% or more. Hence, this proposed technology for pre-sowing treatments is extremely simple and does not require extra energy costs or manual labour. Certainly, power is provided from a modulator 12-volt car battery, while the inoculum may be in any container and of any number. The time for seed treatment - 11 minutes. So, the uniqueness of this technology lies in its application across divergent agronomic conditions.

Technology endorsing decisions and acts:

1. Institute of Plant Physiology. Timiryazev Moscow ANSSR
2. Institute of Chemical Physics. Semenov Moscow ANSSR
3. Agricultural Academy. Timiryazev Moscow
4. Tashkent State University
5. Institute of Rice Uzbekistan
6. NGO Grain, Bean and Crops of the Agricultural Sciences (Orel)

7. All-Union Selections and Genetics Institute of Agricultural Sciences (Odessa)
8. Russian branch of the All-Union Research Institute of Phytopathology MA (Tambov)
9. SANIIRI (Tashkent).
10. SRI cotton MA (Tashkent).
11. Research Institute of cotton breeding and seeds named after G.S. Zaytsev (Tashkent).
12. The Ministry of Agriculture of Kazakhstan, Almaty (Astana) and other scientific institutions.
13. National Centre for Agricultural Research of Kazakhstan.
14. Research Institute of Grain Farming named after Baraev, Shortandy Akmola region.
15. The State Enterprise "North-Kazakhstan Experimental Station" Chagly city.
16. Chelyabinsk Agricultural Research Institute of the Russian Academy of Agricultural Sciences and Business.
17. Kotanay Agricultural Research Institute.
18. "Elite seeds of Tatarstan", Kazan.
19. Deutshe-Russisches Instityt fur Biomagnettische Kybernetik und Nanoteshnologie, Berlin.
20. Agro University named after Suleiman Dimerel of Sparta, Turkey.
21. B Research Institute of Ukraine, Uzbekistan, Tajikistan.

Technology implemented on the premises:
1. Russia and Ukraine (with agricultural farm "Sunny" Simferopol region 1430 ha\ "Engels" Berezonskogo district of Mykolayiv region, 100 hectares, with agricultural farm "Gornoschitsky" Sverdlovsk region, 100 hectares, with agricultural farm "Vladimir" 520ga Krasnoyarsk Territory).
2. Kazakhstan (s /s "Friendship" Kurgoldzhinskogo Akmola region 1000 ha area, s /s Akdalinski Arys district SKO 400ga, PC "Shaproshty"

PC "Navoi" PC "Kara-Tobe" PC "Victory" SKO Sairam district - the total area 4200ga). Arkalyk, Alsantagaysky, Zhaksynsky, Turgay region Kiyminsky areas - total area 100.000ga. Kyzyl-Orda region - 370 ha. Akmola region (Shortandy, Atbasar, Tselinograd, Sandyktau areas) -40 000 ha., Kostanai oblast -10 000 ha., North Kazakhstan -7000 ha.

3. Uzbekistan (100 ha Kashkadarya, Syrdarya 38.000ga, 916ga Bukhara, Namangan 4100ga, Tashkenskaya 44ga, Jizzakh 3000ga areas). The technology proposed by its scientific novelty, reliability and the relevance of research results, economic benefit for Kazakhstan (Akmola region 120 million. 210 thousand. Tenge prices October 2000) and Uzbekistans effect of 364.4 mln. UZS 1997 prices. This differs significantly from the technology of the world's leading groups.

The test results of this research in agricultural fields with different climatic conditions and in the areas of risk farming showed the following benefits:

1. No manual labour in the preparation of planting material.
2. Information exposure occurs directly at the level of the physiology and biochemistry of plants without affecting or modifying their genetics.
3. Germination high.
4. The convergence of results and high crop yields.
5. No ecological load on the environment.
6. Warranty and environmentally friendly production of food biochemically.
7. Independence of limiting environmental factors (heat, cold, lack of moisture, and others.) Minimum.
8. Impact of agricultural pests and weeds insignificant.

Figure 13. Growth and development cobs of corn "Zea mays L." varieties Altyn-739.

a) In experimental control plots,

b) development of stems and cobs of corn. Experience under action of the low EMF

Figure 14. The development of root hairs
a) - under the influence of the low EMF (magnification × 10);
b) - in the absence of low EMF control

EPM root 1

Element	By weight%	Atomic%
N	13.92	14.18
O	43.49	38.80
Na	0.03	0.02
Mg	0.32	0.19
Si	0.42	0.21
P	0.24	0.11
S	0.14	0.06
Cl	0.82	0.33
K	2.18	0.79
Ca	0.35	0.12
Fe	0.09	0.02
Co	0.00	0.00

EPM root 2

Element	By weight%	Atomic%
N	13.92	14.18
O	43.49	38.80
Na	0.03	0.02
Mg	0.32	0.19
Si	0.42	0.21
P	0.24	0.11
S	0.14	0.06
Cl	0.82	0.33
K	2.18	0.79
Ca	0.35	0.12
Fe	0.09	0.02
Co	0.00	0.00

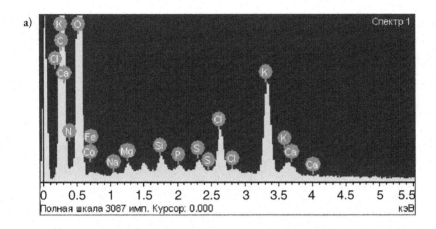

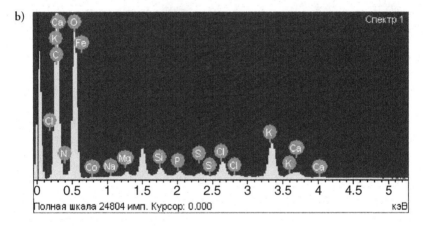

Figure 15 Chromatographic part of the root system of corn "Zea mays L." varieties Altyn-739.

a) in the tillering phase,

b) in the phase of milky stage

Figure 16. Left cobs with seeds that were processed
LF EMF, right – control

The Coordination Centre of the project "Improving the competitiveness of agricultural products" supported this work. We express our heartfelt thanks to the well-known astrophysicist, Head of the Laboratory of the Moon and the planets of the Astrophysical Institute. V.G. Fesenkov, Professor V.G. Teyfelyu, for being of such great assistance in the preparation of this monograph.

The advantages of the proposed technology:

- The possibility of adjusting those properties of the biological object embedded in it by nature;
- Reception of new properties of bio-systems, which were (previously) considered impossible;
- High yields, without polluting the environment, without significant material or energy costs;
- It requires little manual labour and only complements existing agricultural practices, guides;

- Technology has high industrialization – allowing a speedy handling of any batch of seeds designed for unlimited acreage;
- Acceleration of the ripening seeds from different crops in the preparation of the seed.

Independent examination by KazAgroEKS, Institute of Grain and Farming named after A. Baraev, while experimental stations in Chelyabinsk, Kotanay, and Petropavlovsk (Chagly) have shown:

- The growth of quality indicators (2-8 units of gluten, Vitreous 10-20 units; nature 50-80 units. Average);
- Increase crop yields by 20 to 50% compared to control crops;
- Improving the reproductive properties of the seed.

The Analysis of the results of work in the Republic of Uzbekistan in 1996-1998.
(Urinbaev T., Toksanov N.)

We particularly note the effectiveness of the impact of the electromagnetic modulator for seed cotton in 2014 – suggesting a widespread adoption of this technology on cotton farms in Kazakhstan. The following are the results of the modulator in the Republics of Uzbekistan and Tajikistan in the period of 1991-1998.

On the basis of minutes recorded during a meeting of representatives from the Ministry of Agriculture and the private firm "Suvchi-TMB" 31/01/1996 it was decided to start a large-scale three-year laboratory and field tests of this new technology as part of the state tests.

In the first stage of this long-term programme for the implementation of the (suggested) technology in 1996, the territory of Syrdarya region covered the volume of work. For these purposes, the State Production programmes agreed with the relevant authorities. In this project, therefore, the main provisions and recommendations for work in Syrdarya region have been completely confirmed in practice.

This planned project in 1996 undertook the pre-sowing of seed cotton with a subsequent seeding of farms in the territories of Syrdarya, Bukhara and the Namangan regions – with a total area of 41.286 ha. On the basis of prior economic agreements to conduct work involving 92 farms. Thusly, this work was carried out as agreed with the management of the areas and under the supervision of the Ministry of Agriculture of the Republic of Uzbekistan. Furthermore, scientific tests were conducted at the Research Institute of cotton growing technology and the research institutes for cotton breeding and seed named after G.S. Zaytsev and SANIIRI. Comparative tests of treated and untreated seeds were also carried out according to the procedure agreed with the Institute of breeding and seed named after G.S. Zaytsev: Institute of Cotton. On the experimental and control fields, full observation regarding the energy of germination of seeds, plant growth, the accumulation of boxes, conducted surveys cotton yield, the determination of quality, as well as economic and technological features of the fiber was undertaken. Regular surveys and observations confirmed the high energy of cotton in July 1996 - the treated plants themselves being indicators ahead of control on 30-38%. This effect was higher in fields where normal agricultural machinery was used. The grand total for all areas confirmed the favourable forecasts. The average yield of cotton in the treated areas was higher by 5.63 hwt / ha or 20.81%, while the ripening period of cotton was reduced by an average of 10 - 15 days. Hence, an improvement in the technological properties of the fibers and increase in the weight of the seeds was detected. The resulting economic impact in 1996 prices on three areas totalled 327,915,000 in sum.

In 1997, more extensive production was carried out and further research on the technology selected varieties, as well as cereals and other s / crops in different climatic conditions of the Republic of Uzbekistan, undertaken. It was carried out as research on the ETC Institute cotton for testing 12 of the most promising ways for pre-sowing treatment. In an informative report on this subject a positive response was given to electromagnetic seed treatment.

It marked the largest acceleration in obtaining seedlings, outstripping the growth and development of plants, as well as the accumulation of boxes. Counts harvest of raw cotton have shown that if collected on the control of 22.0 hwt / ha, in the form of electromagnetic seed treatment harvest reached 27.8 hwt / ha; further raised to 5.8 hwt / ha, or 26.3% more in comparison with the control - chemical seed dressing.

The above is based on the decision of the Ministry of Agriculture 25.12.1996 STC at the Institute of Cotton Breeding and Seed named after G.S. Zaytsev in 1997 and 1998. Additional studies were conducted to identify the possible of splitting cotton plants and the loss of varietal characteristics and qualities. Observations and surveys confirmed a clear enough picture of the sensitivity of genotypes to electromagnetic seed treatment. Mutagenic effects on heredity after seed treatment in 1996 and 1997 and in 1998 had been feared, but on the contrary, there was a preservation and improvement of cotton yields with more qualitative indicators as compared to control.

During the study period in the control varieties yield, "Namangan- 77" in the first year of the study on the control of results, this figure 30.7 hwt / ha, the experience - 35.1 hwt / ha was recorded. For the six-month period of the dormancy cycle, a "pilot batch" of seeds was left in control for further processing in order to identify the effects on cleavage and deviation from the standard. The results showed: the inspection lot, seeded on a small plot experiment, gave a yield of 41.2 hwt / ha, further treated seeds of the party gave even greater boost yields - 46.6 hwt / ha. From this, we can conclude that the annual treatment of the same seeds can achieve a real yield gain of over 50% in two years and above. Despite the fact that working with this material was suspended, our experts believe that in 3-4 years the processing of the same seed can achieve yields of 70-80 hwt / ha.

Carried over three years, the studies showed that the cottonseeds treated EMM have high vigour and field germination, i.e. an observer sees successful seeds from class to class. Further laboratory tests and production tests carried out in 1998-1999, steadily showed positive results for all performance indicators. Upon completion of successful tests at a meeting of the State Seed Seminar of the Ministry of Agriculture and Water Resources of the Republic of Uzbekistan (with the participation of national entities, and Glavka Uzgossemkontroltsentr), the Ministry of Agriculture and Water Resources of the Republic agreed on the success of this project. It summed up the widespread introduction of advanced high technologies in the Republic of Uzbekistan.

Findings from the state tests:

- According to estimates by the Ministry of Finance of the Republic, profitability from this technology was 2.000%;
- In agreement with the owner of the technology (due to the difficult economic situation in the country) the cost of processing these seeds has been identified at 5% of profits (in a yield increase of 5.6 hwt / ha).

In 1999, according to the results of work with grain crops and cotton, the following was obtained:

Final conclusions - Head of cotton growing and legumes on the effectiveness of this technology;

- Finally, Uzgoskomsemkontroltsentra signed the S. Kuzibaev certification on this technology in the Republic of Uzbekistan;
- Finally, the chief expert of Science in the Uzbek Academy of Sciences, Academician Abdullayev, agreed on the effectiveness of the technology.

Analysis of the results of work from the Republic of Tajikistan
(Urinbaev T., Toksanov N.)

In 1993, Kairakkum agro-industrial enterprise "Mile", a subsidiary of the company "Suvchi-TMB," held in the collective farm named after Kalinin Asht (Leninabad region) an experimental pre-sowing modulator for cotton seed varieties "Kyrgyzstan-3", "Namangan-77", 6524 that was sown across an area of 100 hectares. Sowing in 1993 in the country took place very late, almost a month late, due to a prolonged cold spring. Overall, comparative tests of treated and untreated seeds were carried out according to the procedure agreed with the Institute of breeding and seed named after G.S. Zaytsev and the Institute of cotton. Both the experimental and control fields were in full observation of the energy of seed germination, plant growth, the accumulation of boxes, etc - all being registered before the end of May. In such critical conditions, the technology has proved successful.

Shoots on experimental fields were 3-4 days earlier than the control, regarding all three varieties. Experts noted the collective farm proactive in the development of plants for these experimental crops. Activities eventually leading to early, seven days, maturing cotton. The increase in yield was an average of 3-4 hwt / ha. In addition to the growth was an increase in quantitative characteristics and qualitative indicators, in particular, to an increase in the number and weight of seedpods.

In 1994, experts of agro-industrial enterprise "Mile" held pre-sowing seed cotton on an area of 8500 hectares in the collective Kanibadam, Asht, Nauskogo, and Jabbar-Rasulov and Zafarabad areas, Leninabad region. The work covered nine leading farms in five districts of the region. All farms immediately noted the effective impact of electromagnetic treatment that could be "seen" regarding seed germination and subsequent phases of plant development. Seeded varieties were the most diverse: "An-Bayaut", "Namangan-77", "FV-3", and "Kirghiz-3" 6524.6532. Overall, the results can be summarized as follows: the germination of treated seeds for 2-3 days before - in all phases of the test plants ahead of control. The average increase in yield on all farms was 04.05 hwt / ha. The resulting effect being from the introduction of new technology (in monetary terms) has been very significant. For example, the farm named after 40 Oktyabrya Nauskogo district on an area of 500 hectares, the overall effect amounted to 80 million Russian rubles at the purchase price of the state in 1994. Hence, the project on the Leninabad region has been completed with positive results.

Analysis of works to improve crop yields by an electromagnetic modulation in Russian Federation and Ukraine
(Mingulov I.G., Urinbaev T., Kasymbekov S.)

These territories used a prototype of our technology, which is also called electromagnetic modulator (T.U. Urinbaev modulator Faust-4C).

The farm "Sunny" of the Simferopol region in 1989, when growing winter barley on an area of 730 ha, and winter wheat on the area of 700 ha, the following results were recorded: particularly in the drought. As a result of a pre-sowing treatment modulator, it was hoped to obtain an increase in yield of more than 30% of the gluten in grains 26, 7%, and an excellent quality of bread. Indeed, the bread volume of 100 g flour was 1,300 ml with the growth of the crumb in points a little less than 5 with an overall score of 4.7 - points in the bread (according to the All-Union selection and Genetics Institute).

The farm "Gornoschitsky" Sverdlovsk region in 1989 for corn silage on an area of 100 hectares - as a result of the modulator - obtained an increase in yield of 75 hwt / ha, which accounted for 30% of the economic benefit plan production. When growing corn for silage at the farm "Vladimir" of the Krasnoyarsk Territory in 1989 on an area of 520 ha, it noted an increase in yield of 58 hwt / ha.

These positive results led to the publication of the order № 145 from March 1992, wherein the Minister of Agriculture of the Russian Federation V. Hlistunov, states all the territories, regions and republics of the Russian Federation shall carry out in 1992 and 1994 the "processing electromagnetic modulator ... before sowing seeds and planting material".

Work to introduce these advanced technologies (conducted through a limited liability partnership) was identified by technical and financial resources as necessary. But the methods used by seed treatment proved ineffective. Therefore, the Minister's order was cancelled and further implementation of the technology has been discontinued.

Analysis of works to improve crop yields by an electromagnetic modulation in Kazakhstan

(In Akmolinsk district – Strechenyuk V., Ashirov D., Ashirov R., Mirsaidov R., in Kostanay district – Temirbaev M.A., Serikbaev B.A., Makashev S.N., in Almaty district – Nadirov N.K., Solodova E.V., Ostrovsky N.V., Kozhahmetov N.K., Istaev A.I., in Kyzylorda district – Ashimov S., Dushaev A., Kasymbekov S., Marasulov A., in Petropavl district – Ashirov D.A., Ashirov R.A., in South Kazakhstan district – Abdikerov K., Umbetaev I.I., Bigaraev O.)

When using a prototype of the proposed technology in conditions of severe drought in the Tselinograd area at the farm "Druzhba" Kurgaldzhino area in 1990 wherein cultivation of wheat varieties in the spring "Saratov-29" in an area of 1000 hectares (of crops) increased to 100%.

The farm "Akdalinski" Arys district of Tashkent region in 1990 winter wheat varieties "Red Water" on an area of 400 hectares after the application of the prototype EMM to increase yield was 58%.

In 1995, KC "Care" work carried out a preliminary treatment of wheat seeds in the territory Torgai area in Arkalyk, Amontagayskom, Zhaksynskom Kiyminskom areas and total area of 100 000 hectares. Sowing the company in 1995 in the field Torgai was very late. The reason for this was a lack of fuel, machinery, seeds, spare parts, etc. In these extreme conditions, our technology has proved successful. All 13 collective farms obtained positive results. Experienced crops to sprout 1-2 days before the test crop, and germination was 10-40% higher than in the control fields. Specialists in the sector of observations during the growing season indicated that in all phases of development modulator treated wheat was ahead of untreated plants. The general condition of the test plants, including the root system, being much higher than in the controls. As a result, on experimental fields, wheat ripened 6-7 days earlier than in the controls field. According to test results, the biological difference in yield between the experimental and control crops ranged from 2 to 8 g / ha. According to the results of separate harvesting difference in yields ranged from 20 to 80%, which is considered to be very effective in an area of 100 hectares - as a result of risky agriculture. Osnavnaya seeded varieties were "Saratov-29", "Tselinnaya-Anniversary" and "Bezenchukskaya-129". According to the Department of Agriculture Torgai area, precisely those areas where our technology has been used, were the first in an overall harvest and yield.

In 1998-2000 PC "Karatobe", "Shapyrashty", "victory", "Alisher Navoi" South Kazakhstan region tested wheat varieties "Bezostaya-1" and "Red Water-210." All households received an additional harvest from the 31 to 60 percent. Moreover, the gluten content in test samples were minus 10.0-20,0% in all the households.

Atbasar, Sandyktau and Shortandy, 12 farms: TOO "Niva", LLP "Aral-Tobe", LLP "Bektau", LLP "Spaska", LLP "Ulan", LLP "Wide", LLP "Amantay", LLP "Sandyktau -2 ", LLP" Rodina ", LLP" merry ", LLP" Podlesnoe ", LLP" Azat "noticed an increase to the yield ranging from 30% or more. In value terms, prices in November 2000 (per ton of 3-grade softest wheat - 10 000 tenge). This increase amounted to about 144 million tenge, or US $ 1 million.

Various studies show that essentially only precision adaptive agro technologies possess the greatest biological effectiveness. For example, in the year's 2005- 2007 the authors, together with German scientists conducted comprehensive studies of advanced technologies for different crops (wheat, soybean, sugar beet).

GRAVITON Bio Energie.

Deutsch-Russisches Institut für Biomagnetische Kybernetik und Nanotechnologie

Высокоточные, адаптивные нано и электро-магнитные агротехнологии в растениеводстве, животноводстве и птицеводстве.

Комплексные органические вытяжки из сапропеля.

Биогенные наночастицы металлов.

Электромагнитная обработка растительных объектов.

Berlin 2008

For the first time in the practice of APC, we offered in a single technological cycle, to repeatedly prove (in the field adaptive agricultural technologies in crop production), results in three areas:

Различные исследования и наш накопленный опыт в АПК показывает, что в основном только высоточные, адаптивные агратехнологии обладают наибольшей биологической эффективностью, экологичностью и могут гарантировать стабильный высокий урожай сельхозпроизводителям при минимальной зависимости от лимитирующих природных факторов – жара, холод, переизбыток или недостаток влаги.

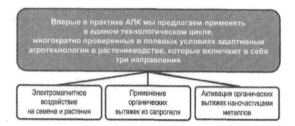

В чем суть и преимущество адаптивных агротехнологий ?

Характерной особенностью адаптивных агротехнологий является механизм их воздействия на раститильный организм и окружающую среду, посредством выбора оптимальных режимов и средств реализации этого воздействия.

Воздействие происходит непосредственно на физиологию и биохимические процессы раститильного объекта, не затрагивая и не модифицирую при этом генетику самих растений.

Используя такие технологии мы производим, например, органические нанорегуляторы роста растений с параметрами, обеспечивающие стабильные урожаи при учете лимитирующих природных условий и снижающими экологическую нагрузку на окружающую среду.

1. Electromagnetic effects on seeds and plants
2. The use of organic extracts of sapropel
3. Activation of organic extracts of metal nanoparticles

A characteristic feature of adaptive agricultural technologies is the mechanism of their effects on the plant and the environment, by choosing the optimal modes and means of implementation of this action.

Exposure takes place directly on the physiology and biochemical processes of the plant object, without affecting or modifying the genetics of the plants themselves.

Using such technology, such as organic Nano regulatory plant growth parameters providing stable yields, taking into account the limiting environmental conditions and reducing the environmental burden on the environment, yields increase.

Table 2 The results of the introduction of the pre-sowing treatment technology by Professor Ashirov A.M., with employees in various farms in Kazakhstan and abroad

					WHEAT		
Farms, year	Parameters	Frequency, Hz	Magnetic field strength, μ V/cm^2	Duration	Productivity of land, Control, ql./ha	Productivity of land, Experiment, ql./ha	Increase in yield,%
1	2	3	4	5	6	7	8
1991 year. Chimkent region Arysky area Akadalinsk farm Kazakhstan	The tidal forces of gravity	14	20	10	7,2	12,6	+75%
1992 year. Tulkin,Uzbekistan	-//-//-	14	20	10			

Farms, year	Parameters	Frequency, Hz	Magnetic field strength, μ V/cm^2	Duration	WHEAT		
					Productivity of land, Control, ql./ha	Productivity of land, Experiment, ql./ha	Increase in yield,%
1	2	3	4	5	6	7	8
1996 year. Syrdarinsky area. Gulam farm, Uzbekistan	The tidal forces of gravity, the influence of the sun.	14	20	11	26,3	47,6	+180%
1999 year. Sairam region, PK «Pobeda», Kazakhstan	-//-//-	14	20	11	19,7	25,9	+31%
1999 year. Sairam region, PK «Kara-Tobe», Kazakhstan	-//-//-	14	20	11	23,7	37,2	+57%
1999 year. Sairam region, PK «Navoi», Kazakhstan	-//-//-	14	20	11	17,0	27,2	+60%
2000 year. Tashkent region. «Kim Pen Hva» Uzbekistan	-//-//-	14	20	11	45,8 54,4 46,8	58,0 70,8 53,1	+26,6% +30,1% +13,4%
					44,3 38,3 45,0	56,0 48,4 53,9	+26,6% +26,3% +19,7%
2000 year. Navoisky region. Kzyltep district, Uzbekistan	-//-//-	14	20	11	32,7	40,3	+23%
2000 year. Novobah district Uzbekistan	-//-//-	14	20	11	40,8	53,5	+31%
2000 year. Navoisky region. Uzbekistan	-//-//-	14	20	11	34,4	44,2	+28,5%

Farms, year	Parameters	Frequency, Hz	Magnetic field strength, µ V/cm²	Duration	WHEAT		
					Productivity of land, Control, ql./ha	Productivity of land, Experiment, ql./ha	Increase in yield,%
1	2	3	4	5	6	7	8
2000 year. Hatyrchin district,Uzbekistan	-//-//-	14	20	11	30,8	38,5	+25%
2000 year. Akmolisnkaya region, Kazakhstan «Agrocenter Astana»:							
LLP «Niva» № 20	-//-//-	14	20	11	33,5	46,2	37,9%
LLP «Niva» № 21	-//-//-	14	20	11	17,2	20,4	18,6%
LLP «Aral-Tobe»	-//-//-	14	20	11	11,3	16,0	+41,6%
LLP «Bektau» № 31	-//-//-	14	20	11	18,9	22,2	+17,5%
TOO «Bektau» № 94	-//-//-	14	20	11	10,4	19,2	+84,6%
LLP «Spaskoe»	-//-//-	14	20	11	20,4	21,3	+4,4%
LLP «Ulan» № 31	-//-//-	14	20	11	14,0	27,2	+94%
LLP «Ulan» № 29	-//-//-	14	20	11	13,5	20,0	+48%
LLP «Shirokoe»	-//-//-	14	20	11	15,9	18,5	+16%
«Amantai» № 30	-//-//-	14	20	11	8,4	12,2	+45%
«Amantai» № 72	-//-//-	14	20	11	16,9	21,6	27,8%
«Sandiktau» 2 № 10	-//-//-	14	20	11	6,9	11,3	+63,7%
«Rodina»	-//-//-	14	20	11	10,6	15,8	+49%
LLP «Veseloe»	-//-//-	14	20	11	10,3	13,5	+31%
«Azat»	-//-//-	14	20	11	15,5	26,8	+72,9%

Farms, year	Parameters	Frequency, Hz	Magnetic field strength, µ V/cm²	Duration	WHEAT		
					Productivity of land, Control, ql./ha	Productivity of land, Experiment, ql./ha	Increase in yield,%
1	2	3	4	5	6	7	8
2001 year. Chelyab-inskSRIOA (rye),Russia	-//-//-	14	20	11	40,2	44,8	+11%
2002 year. North-Kazakh-stan region, experimental station	-//-//-	14	20	11	15,9	19,1	+20%
2002 year. LLP «LEVT» Kazakhstan	-//-//-	14	20	11	17,0	22,9	+34%
2002 year. Kostanay region, Selantevsky district,LLP «Churakovsky»	-//-//-	14	20	11	11,8	14,2	20,34%
2003 year. Kyzylorda region Zhalagash district LLP «Shamenov»	-//-//-	14	20	11	42,4	50,5	21,5
2004 year. Akmolinskaya region RPA «Union of Farmers of Kazakhstan» Farmer Sagymabev	-//-//-	14	20	11	Sprouts from 1m² 220	Sprouts from 1m² 300	Difference 80
2004 year Akmolinskaya region RPA «Union of Farmers of Kazakhstan» Farmer Krugelchuk	-//-//-	14	20	11			

					WHEAT		
Farms, year	Parameters	Frequency, Hz	Magnetic field strength, μ V/cm²	Duration	Productivity of land, Control, ql./ha	Productivity of land, Experiment, ql./ha	Increase in yield,%
1	2	3	4	5	6	7	8
2004 year. Akmolinskaya region RPA «Union of Farmers of Kazakhstan» Farmer Suraev V.	-//-//-	14	20	11	Sprouts from 1m² 230	Sprouts from 1m² 300	Difference 70
2005 year. Kyzylorda region Shieli district LLP «Shieli-Avangard»	-//-//-	14	20	11			
2006 year. Akmolinskaya region. Esilsky district, Razdolnoe village LLP «Garysh»	-//-//-	14	20	11	12	16,7	39%
2006 year. Akmolinskaya region, Sandyktausky district, Bogoslovka village LLP «Bogoslovka»	-//-//-	14	20	11	Sprouts from 1m² 223	Sprouts from 1m² 379	Difference 156
2007 year. Akmolinskay region, Esilsky district, Razdolnoe village LLP «Garysh»	-//-//-	14	20	11	12	17	41%
2004 year. Suleiman Demirel University Sparta city Turkey					Laboratory tests on wheat	The results are positive	

Farms, year	Parameters	Frequency, Hz	Magnetic field strength, µ V/cm²	Duration	WHEAT		
					Productivity of land, Control, ql./ha	Productivity of land, Experiment, ql./ha	Increase in yield,%
1	2	3	4	5	6	7	8
Deutsche-Russishes Institut fur Biomagnetische Kybernetik und Nanotechnologie Berlin 2008		14	20	11			21,3%
«Elite seeds of Tatarstan, Kazan,2009» Association		14	20	11	32	41	9,28%

Farms,year	Parameters	Frequency, Hz	Magnetic field strength, µ V/cm²	Duration	COTTON		
					Productivity of land, Control, ql./ha	Productivity of land, Experiment, ql./ha	Increase in yield,%
1	2	3	4	5	6	7	8
1996 year. Namangsky region k/h Uchkurgan, Uzbekistan	-//-//-	14	20	11	30,1	37,6	+25%
1996 year. Institute named after Zaycev, Uzbekistan	-//-//-	14	20	11 15 21	30,7	35,1 33,5 27,5	14% 11% 11%
1997 year. Tashkentskaya district Iik-Ota farm, Uzbekistan	-//-//-	14	20	11	22,8	31,5	+38%
1998 year. Farizhskaya region Naimancha Farm, Uzbekistan	-//-//-	14	20	11	18,0	24,0	+33,3%

Farms,year	Parameters	Frequency, Hz	Magnetic field strength, µ V/cm²	Duration	COTTON		
					Productivity of land, Control, ql./ha	Productivity of land, Experiment, ql./ha	Increase in yield,%
1	2	3	4	5	6	7	8
2001 г. Navoisky region. Uzbekistan: Hatyrchinskydistrict	-//-//-	14	20	11	14,8	24,9	+67,5%
Navbahorsky district	-//-//-	14	20	11	17,0	26,7	+43,5%
Navoisky district	-//-//-	14	20	11	21,8	24,1	+10,5%

Farms,year	Parameters	Frequency, Hz	Magnetic field strength, µ V/cm²	Duration	RICE		
					Productivity of land, Control ql./ha	Productivity of land, Experiment, ql./ha	Increase in yield,%
1	2	3	4	5	6	7	8
2000 year. Kyzyl-Ordinskaya region «Dostyk»	-//-//-	14	20	11	48,7	5,5	+34,5
2001 year. Kyzyl-Ordinskaya region Zhanakorgansky district Tugusken farm					38,5	6,6	+21.0

All data for preliminary treatment and yields are given in these tables.

In addition to the low-frequency modulator "NEMI - 15" in the fields of the Akmola region, we studied the effect obtained by using different electromagnetic emitters (ultrasonic treatment, the emitter of the ultraviolet spectrum, infrared emitter, radio waves, X-rays, etc).

Example 1. Shortandy area. LLP "Bektau." 2000 Wheat - sort of "Kazakhstan - Jubilee" field № 24. The period of processing selected seed for the position of the Moon in the sign of Capricorn. All timed locally, of course, according to a seasonal time schedule. Processing was performed for 10 minutes. Following which, selected periods characterized by the minimum values of tidal forces and the maximum intensity of the M regions of the Sun, were confirmed by data obtained from the Internet.

As can be seen from Table. 1, the best results and EMM processing methods infrared spectra are clearly shown. The increase in yields even under drought conditions (in summer, there is not a drop of rain), varies by 95 and 70%, respectively.

Example 2.

In 1999, LLC "Topaz" Shortandy district in the Akmola region (after the removal of the party harvest) was selected for its wheat varieties "Omsk-27", which had been treated for 10 minutes in a low frequency electromagnetic field (LF EMM) with a wavelength of 10th - 105m and a frequency of 10 Hz oscillations. Then, the said party was covered for storage as a seed.

Table 3. The results of the influence of various electromagnetic radiation ranges on wheat yield

Type of treatment	The length of the wave, m	Productivity, ql./ha	Note
Control	No treatment	4	Low yield due to severe drought 2000 year.
Ultrasonic treatment	$(1.5-10^{7} -1,5 \cdot 10^{4}$ m)	4,1	
UltravioletTreatment	$(10^{-7} - 10^{-9}$ m)	6,0	
Low frequency electromagnetic generator	$(10^{-1} - 10^{-11}$ m)	7.8	
Treatment by infrared emitter	$(10^{4} - 10^{-6}$ m)	6.8	
Обработка излучателем инфракрасного диапазона			

Type of treatment	The length of the wave, m	Productivity, ql./ha	Note
Radio waves treatment	(1-10^5 m)	4,2	
The X-ray treatment	(10^{-8} – 10^{-11} m)	3,2	

In 2000, this party was a subjected wheat seedbed handling low-frequency electromagnetic fields in a similar mode.

Selection and definition of the projection time period in the area of crop processing being performed as in Example 1. After processing, the batch wheat was sown on a third day from field № 21.

To control the two parties, wheat of similar varieties was sown: one without treatment and one with pre-plant treatment from a low frequency electromagnetic generator (EMM) in the same mode. As such, the yield data obtained in 2000, the LP "Topaz" of Shortandy district in the Akmola region on number 21, as well as data from the control fields are shown in Table. 1. These test results being confirmed by a certificate from the Inter-departmental Commission of the Republic of Kazakhstan on 20.09.2000.

Table 4.

Type of treatment	Productivity (Experiment), ql./ha	Biological (control), productivity, ql./ha	Difference (experiment-control), (addition), ql./ha
No treatment	-	4.0	4.0
Presowing treatment, EMM,10 Hz, 10 min	30.2	23,6	6.6
Provisional (EMM, 10 Hz,10 min) and presowing (EMM, 10 Hz,10 min) treatment	36.8	23,6	13,2

Table 4 shows the importance of the pre-treatment for a seedbed. The increase amounted to (13.2 - 6.6) = 6.6 hwt / ha.

Example 3.

Interestingly, on July 15, 2000 in the village of Marinovka Atbasar in Akmola region, both the control and experimental field (number 4) was subjected to a "test" group of locusts: behaving in the manner of an "Italian Prussian". At 10 hr. 15 mins, these locusts, in approximately equal amounts ("100 - 150 pieces per 1m2) were driven on to the experimental and control fields. At 11 hr. 30 mins, they were "encouraged" to "migrate" to the experimental field. By 12 hr. 15 mins, however, about 90% of these locusts were on control field, while about 10% - were on the trial field. At 12 hr. 45 minutes, the locusts left the experimental field.

Now, an analysis of wheat stalks in the laboratory of the Institute of Chemical Physics. NN Semenov of the Russian Academy of Sciences (laboratory of Professor B.R. Shub) revealed the presence of tannins traces on the stems of plants within the experimental field.

Tannins, of course, are known to have a strong insecticidal action. Hence, the processing mode was similar to Example 1. This example shows that any treatment by these inventive methods has an impact at a cellular level and, as a result, plants acquire protection from pests.

Example 4.

On May 25, 2000 at 23 hr. 30 min. local time in the village of Shirokoe in the Sandyktau district of Akmola region, selected areas were treated with cucumber seeds varieties "Nizhynsky", which were planted on the 2nd day after treatment in the control and experimental fields of 0.1 ha. As such, the treatment of cucumber seeds was carried out through a low-frequency electromagnetic field in a mode similar to that of Example 1.

Presented in the Table 3, therefore, is data showing that the treatment of these cucumber seeds (by a low-frequency electromagnetic field) reduces the ripening period of 9 days and increases the yield of the culture to 4.9 per hectare.

Example 5.

The farm "Krasnaya Zvezda" in Dzhetysay district in the South Kazakhstan region on May 2, 1992, had processed cotton seeds (through a low-frequency electromagnetic field), sown in the manner of Example 1. Indeed, these cotton seeds were sown for 2-3 days after treatment.

Analysis of the data shows that the treated cotton yield increased by 5.4 hwt / ha. Also, seed germination was 3-4 days earlier than in the control box.

Test results with cucumber seeds shown in Table 5.

№ п/п		Experimental sowing, ha	Control sowing, ha	Difference between experiment and control
1	Sowing Area	0,1	0,1	-
2	Germination date	31 May 2000	28 May 2000	3 days earlier
3	Ripening date	12 July 2000	3 July 2000	9 days earlier
4	Productivity ql./ha			490 kg greater

The results of the experiments are given in Table 6.

№ п/п	Variant	The height of the plant, cm	The number of fruit branches, pc.	The number of boxes, pc.	Productivity, ql./ha	Addition ql./ha
11	Control	91,4	12,8	6,5	40,1	0
22	Experiment	94,9	13,6	7,3	45,5	+ 5,4

Despite the lack of water for irrigation and pesticide seed treatment in the growing season on these experimental fields, it was observed that gumoza disease, wilt and root rot were reduced. The maturing cotton in the experimental fields started at 7-10 days earlier than in the controls.

Example 6.

In the farm "Dostyk" of the Kyzylorda district of fields in the Syrdarya region, in 2000 on May 5 at 8:30, seeds of rice variety "Marjane" were treated by a low-frequency electromagnetic field in conditions similar to Example 1.

The processing period and local time were determined from Figure 7. Moreover, rice seeds were sown for 2-3 days after treatment by conventional agronomic methods. The resulting analysis of plants, stalks densities and yields of the rice variety "Akmarzhan" EMM being processed on the farm "Dostyk" of the Kyzylorda region in 2000.

Now, any analysis of the data in Table 7 shows that a pre-sowing treatment of rice seeds in a low-frequency electromagnetic field can increase yields by an average of 15-16 hwt / ha. Thus, when analysing examples 1-6, one discovers that the effectiveness of the impact on seeds (proposed by these methods) is provided by an approximation to the optimal value of their geomagnetic background. Indeed, the electromagnetic field of the Earth and Sun, weak fluctuations from deep space, as well as the electromagnetic fields used during preliminary and pre-processing techniques, all affect the dynamics of seed biorhythms. So, when they are exposed to electromagnetic fields, seeds "start" to energize. Their energy-resources and nutrient plant cells acting like a renewed "memory", which improves their properties at a genetic level. Enhancing, thereby, their immune systems and increasing their required enzyme composition. As a result, these fields activate the vitality of plants.

Table 7.

Variant "Experiment – Control"	Height of the plant, cm	The Length, см	Main whisk			Empty seeds. %	The Mass, г.	Mass of 1 stalk of straw, g,	Specific mass of grain, %	The mass of 1000 seeds, g	The mass of grain from 1m², g	The number of productive whisks	Productivity, ql./ha
			Number of spikelets										
			Full	Empty	Total								
Experiment	98,6	18,6	88,6	11.2	99,9	11,0	3,12	3,38	48.0	35,6	666,2	210,0	65,5
Control	96,9	17,8	69,3	3,9	79,2	12.5	246	273	47,4	35,5	460,0	187	48,7

The results of the dometrics analysis of plant density and the productivity of stalks of rice varieties "Akmarzhan" as presented in Table 7.

Impacting any seeds electromagnetic field by the methods we propose, will provide an "energy information" surge on biological objects. Indeed, plants "remember" their wild ancestors, organize themselves and restore their drought resistance, along with their ability to resist pests. As such, all of the above leads to increased productivity. Hence, it has been found that after exposure to electromagnetic inoculum in wheat and rice grains, there is a dramatic increase in the content α-, ß- amylase, an average of 20%, which leads to a rapid hydrolysis of starch and dextrin's endosperm,, as well as a sharp increase of mono- and disaccharides in the grain. This culture medium significantly increases in energy shoots. Additionally, within the stalks of wheat, traces of tannin were discovered - having a strong insecticidal action.

Thus, the analysis of "energy information" patterns exchanged in nature have made it possible to identify (by the treatment of seeds and planting material treated through low-frequency electromagnetic fields generated by special modulators), genuinely revolutionary methods within agriculture practice. Certainly, the effect of the modulator provides seed and planting materials with an "additional energy boost," which result in the acceleration of germination, an accelerated growth and development in plants, photosynthesis and the formation of a powerful ventilator - as well as an increased resistance to disease, a lack of moisture in the soil, and TDS.

Legumes and vegetables.

On farm "Temryuk" in the Temryuk district, along with the farm "Dawn" in the Ust-Labinsk district of the Krasnodar region of Russia (in 1990), when growing pea seeds following treatment through a prototype of our modulator, each prepared to increase their seed yield of vegetable pea 3 hwt / ha. In another farm - named after Kotovsky, in the Dnipropetrovsk region - growing peas was planned in an area of 100 hectares. After the application of a

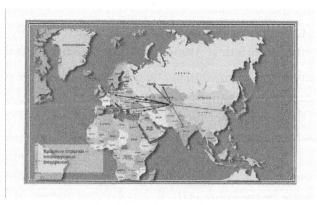

Examination results for the absence of a negative impact on the environment and changes at the genetic level

prototype modulator, however, they obtaining an increase in yield 6 t / ha in an area of 30 hectares - 25 hwt / ha.

Furthermore, in 1992, greenhouse complex № 1 of Tashkent (after processing tomato seeds in the area of 0.2 ha) obtained an increase in their harvest of tomatoes by 989 kg - the prices of the first half of 1992 amounting to 19.780 rubles.

1. Siberian Medical University of the Ministry of Health. They thoroughly checked the harmlessness of these processes to the health of operators working with the electromagnetic transmitter and the ecological purity of the environment.
2. Institute of Microbiology, Academy of Sciences of Uzbekistan. The conclusion on the lack of genetic changes in plants was made manifest.
3. Academy of Sciences of Uzbekistan. They concluded there was little influence by the device on any mutagenic changes in plants.
4. JSC "Elite seeds of Tatarstan" Kazan.
5. The Institute of Chemical Physics. Semenov Moscow ANSSR
6. Deutshe-Russisches Instityt fur Biomagnettische Kybernetik und Nanoteshnologie Berlin.

Closing

These tests are research on agricultural fields with different climatic conditions in areas of risk farming: each showing the following benefits:

1. No manual labour in the preparation of planting material.
2. Information exposure occurs directly at the level of the physiology and biochemistry of plants without affecting or modifying their genetics.
3. High germination.
4. The convergence of results and high crop yields.
5. No ecological load on the environment.
6. A warranty on environmentally friendly and biochemically valuable food production.

7. Minimum dependence of limiting environmental factors (heat, cold, lack of moisture, and others.)
8. Impact of agricultural pests and weeds insignificant.

Technology with higher accuracy can:

- Correct and obtain biological properties that were previously hidden within nature;
- Predict probable future results and events;
- Access features and properties of biological systems that were previously thought impossible;
- Get high yields in any part of the world and increase the productivity of any crop without polluting the environment.

REFERENCES

1. Cooke *D.J Cole*з EM. The concept of Lunacy: a review/ // Psychol,Rep. 1978. Vol.42, No 3. Pt. 1. P. *891*-897.
2. Парнов Е. Звездные знаки. М.: Знание, 1984. С. 110-128.
3. *Parnov E.* Star signs. M.: Knowledge, 1984. P. 110-128.
4. *Tallquist K.* Manan I myt och dikt, folketro och kult. Stockholm, 1948. p. 225
5. *Heckert H.* 1 H. Lunationsrhythmen des menschichen Orangismus (methodisches und ergebnisse). Leipzig: Akad.Verl. Gesst and Porti K.G. 1961.
6. *Brezowsky H., Dietel H.* Der Einflib von Wetter und Jahreszeit auf Wehenbeginn, Wehendauer, vorzetigen Blasennensprung und Frahgeburt // Z. Ceb?rtsch.. Gynak. 1967. Bd 166, No 3. 5. 244-271.
7. *Oliven J.F.* Moonlight and Nervous Disorders: A historical study //Amer. J. Psychiat. 1943. Vol. 99. P. 579-584.
8. *Stone M.H.* madness and the moon revisited //Psychiat. Ann. 1976. Vol 6 P.170-176
9. *Gauquelin M.* Cosmic influence on human behavior. New York: Aurora Press., 1985.

10. *Lieber A.L.* On the Moon again //Amer. J, Psychiat.1975. Vol. 132, No 6. P. 669-670.

11. Дубров А.П. Лунные ритмы у человека. М.: Медицина, 1990. 190 с.

12. *Dubrov A.P.* Lunar rhythms in humans. M.: Medicine, 1990. 190 c.

13. *Michel F.c., Dessler A.J., Walter G.K.A* Search for a Correlation between K_p and the Lunar Phase // J. Geophys. Res. 1964. Vol. 68, №19. P. 4177-4181.

14. *Максимов И.В., Саруханян Э.И., Смирнов Н.Н.* Океан и космос. Л.: Гидрометеоиздат, 1970. 245 с.

15. Maksimov I.V., Saruhanyan E.I., Smirnov N.N. Ocean and cosmos. L.:

16. Gidrometeoizdat, 1970. p.245

17. *Currie R.* Lunah tides and the wealth of nations // New Sci.1988. Vol. 120, № 1637. P. 52-55.

18. *Картер С.* Королевство приливов/Пер. с англ. Л.: Гидрометеоиздат,1977. 274 с.

19. *Carter S.* The Kingdom of tides/Trans.: Gidrometeoizdat, 1977. P. 274.

20. *Мельхиор П.* Земные приливы /Пер. с англ. М.: Мир, 1968. 178 с.

21. *Melhior P.* Earth tides / Trans.: Mir, 1968. p. 178.

22. Necovetics O. Periodicity of the release of seismic enrhge and the anomalistic great cycles of the moon// Asta geodaet cucle of the moon // Asta gepdaet. Montan Haing 1984. Vol. 19. №3-4. P. 249-255.

23. *Надиров Н.К., Аширов А.М., Инюшин В.М., Онгарбаев Е.С., Солодова Е.В.* Закономерность усиления биорезонансной активации семян сельскохозяйственных культур: Диплом №272 на научное открытие. 14.12.2004.

24. *Nadirov N.K., Ashirov A.M., Inyushin V.M., Ongarbayev E.S., Solodova E.V.* The pattern of amplification of bio-resonance activation of seed crops: Diploma №272 on scientific discovery. 14.12.2004.

25. Патент РК № 15355. Способ обработки семенного и посадочного материала. Национальное патентное ведомство (КАЗПАТЕНТ) / Аширов А.М., Надиров Н.К., Аширов Д.А., Онгарбаев Е С. Алматы, 2004.

26. Patent RK № 15355.A method for processing seed and planting material. National Patent Office (KAZPATENT) / Ashirov A.M., Nadirov N.K., Ashirov D.A., Ongarbayev E.S. Almaty, 2004.

27. Патент РК № 53557. Способ регистрации электрических полей живых объектов. Национальное патентное ведомство (КАЗПАТЕНТ) / Надиров Н.К., Инюшин В.М., Маминова Г.Н., Солодова Е.В.

28. Patent RK № 53557.A method of recording the electrical fields of live objects. National Patent Office (KAZPATENT) / Nadirov N.K., Inyushin V.M., Maminova G.N., Solodova E.V.

29. *Опалинская А.М., Агупова Л.П.* Влияние естественных и искусственных электромагнитных полей на физико-химическую и элементарную биологические системы. Томск: Изд-во Томского ун-та, 1984. 190 с.

30. *Opalinskaya A.M., Agupova L.P.* The impact of natural and artificial electromagnetic fields on physical-chemical and elementary biological systems. Tomsk: TomskUniversityEdition, 1984. p. 190.

31. *Владимирский Б.М.* Возмущения естественного электромагнитного поля Земли в диапазоне сверхнизких частот // Труды Крымского медицинского института. 1973. Т. 53. С. 3-13.

32. *Vladimirsky B.M.* Disturbances of the natural electromagnetic field of the Earth in the range of ultra-low frequencies // Proceedings of the Crimean Medical Institute. 1973. Vol.53. pp. 3-13.

33. Галь *Л.Н.* О механизме действия сверхслабых факторов на живые и модельные системы //VII Международная крымская конференция «Космос и биосфера». Судак, 2007. С. 21-22.

34. Gal L.N. About the mechanism of action of ultra-weak factors on living and modeling systems //VII International Crimean Conference "Cosmos and Biosphere".Sudak, 2007. pp. 21-22.

35. *Лященко А.К.* // Физико-химические свойства водных систем. СПб :Изд-во СПб. ун-та, 1991. С. 29-42.

36. *Lyashenko A.K.* // Physical-chemical properties of aqueous systems. 1991. pp. 29-42.

37. *Давыдов А. С.* Биология и квантовая механика. Киев: Наукова думка 1979. 296с.

38. *Davydov A.S.* Biology and quantum mechanics. Kiev: Naukova dumka 1979. p. 296.
39. Frohlich H.F // Advences in Elektronics and Electron Physics, ed. L.Marton. 1980. V. 53.P.85.
40. http://biophys.msu.ru/coferen/98_tbct/abc158.html
41. *Аксенов С.И., Булычев А.А., Грунина Т.Ю., Туровецкий В.Б.* Влияние низкочастотного магнитного поля на активность эстераз и изменение pH у зародыша в ходе набухания семян пшеницы // Биофизика. 2000. Т. 45. С. 737-745.
42. *Aksenov S.I., Bulychev A.A., Grunina T.U., Turovecki V.B. Impact of low-frequency magnetic fields on the esterase activity and the change in pH in the embryo during the imbibition of seeds // Biophysics. 2000. Vol.45. pp. 737-745.*
43. *Павлович С.А.* Магнитная восприимчивость организмов. Минск: Наука и техника, 1985. 110 с.
44. *Pavlovich S.A.* The magnetic susceptibility of organisms. Minsk: Science and Technology, 1985. p.110
45. *Надиров Н.К., Аширов А.М., Инюшин В.М., Онгарбаев Е.С., Солодова Е.В.* Закономерность усиления биорезонансной активации семян сельскохозяйственных культур: Диплом №272 на научное открытие. 14.12.2004.
46. *Nadirov N.K., Ashirov A.M., Inyushin V.M., Ongarbayev E.S., Solodova E.V.* The pattern of amplification of bio-resonance activation of seed crops: Diploma №272 on Scientific Discovery. 14.12.2004.
47. Patent RK №15355.A method for processing seed and planting material. National Patent Office (KAZPATENT)/Ashirov A.M., Nadirov N.K., Ashirov D.A., Ongarbayev E.S. Almaty, 2004.
48. Sabden O., Ashirov A. The conceptual strategy of humankind'ssurvival in the XXI century and food security // Izvestia NAN RK – 2015 - №2

QUINTESSENCE

New ideas, concepts, researches, techniques stated in this book, as well as their practical implementation, are given below:

1. For the first time in history, a **strategic concept for humankind's survival in the third millennium** has been developed. It is based on principles of good planetary housekeeping and universal civilization in the post-industrial world. A view upholding spirituality, scientific and technical adaptation, ecology, space exploration, economics and world safety as paramount (pages 6-40).Only this system and its coordinated measures (according to six basic elements) can ensure peace and a steady life. The creation and synthesis of these fundamental scientific theories - in various spheres of knowledge and organization – offer a uniform, or creative, process of design for futurity. After all, these components alone profess a philosophy uniting the complete picture of a new civilization world (fig. 1,2,3).

2. As a new methodology connecting the achievements of the natural sciences with the humanization of society, this design fits our planetary house (fig. 2) as it is shown elsewhere. Of course, these scientific and technical advances emphasize an imbalance between the level of knowledge gained and the degree of public spirituality. In this regard, our megaproject is **"About (the) Creation of (a) New Spiritually Technological Cluster "the Turkestan Valley» – a Way to Humanize Society"**. Overall, the purpose behind a transformation of Turkestan into a spiritual centre (megalopolis) of international significance and a revival of Eurasian integration uniting West and East along the Great Silk Way, is obvious. For the first time, therefore, we present an example of how one Central Asian region may progress through melding spiritually with cultural and technological developments (pages 42-58).

3. Now, millions of people in the world live in poverty, while suffering from hunger and deprivation. In recent years, due to an excessive issue of US dollars, the money supply has exceeded the volume of manufactured goods

by 10-12 times. Accordingly, "objective" economic laws have been violated - an imbalance leading towards a crisis. In many rich countries, even new technological achievements only happen for the sake of capital. **Hence, the best universal measurement of currency is in terms of "power", i.e. kilowatts related to currency – kW/currency.** As such, we are rid of speculative capital, which has no real power. (Pages 33-37).

4. Irrespective of our desires, the burning issues of globalization raise fears of mass destruction across the planet. To solve these global macrotasks is not in the power of states, international structures, or institutes. Indeed, we authors consider that this new millennium will witness power (from the point of view of vested interests), gravitating towards a world government: to an international parliament. Of course, separate elements of this world management already exist - the UN, the Kyoto Protocol, etc. Yet, these structures don't react quickly enough in these changing times. Therefore, we the authors consider it time to place before the world community a question – **about global control systems in our forthcoming civilization and the regulation of these world processes** (fig. 3). Certainly, we authors speculate a number of new recommendations require consideration: involving a potential "reformation" of the UN and other international organizations (pages 6-12, 38-40). In this regard, one of us sent a letter with recommendations to the heads of the developed countries of the world (G8, G20).

5. Transitioning from a market economy **to an innovative economy in post-industrial civilization** is reasonable. The rapidity of development being the cornerstone of inquiry. Frustratingly, the largest world organizations practically neglect global economic processes in favour of supporting the "petro-chemical" dollar. However, humanity now seeks for a consciously monitored process, which eliminates the subjective roots of previous market economies. This must be objectively realised, no doubt, pushing national economies into a new system of fiscal activities. Following which, a rational civilized economy will blossom, along with logical forecasting in these processes (pages 6-14, 33-40).

6. Unarguably, an agreeable length of time needs to be given to developed countries so that they may adapt themselves to global principles - not to

mention altering the material aspect of business from immediate gain to a form of spirituality. A problem they specifically face when we consider the abyss between the achievements of science and technology compared to the primitive spiritual life of present day society. Indeed, the cult of material values was always directly linked to the greatest decrease in morality ever recorded. All meaning, we must revive our hearts if we are ever to understanding our place in the Cosmos. Clearly, this is also an attempt to develop a global world outlook. The main task before us being to humanize the thinking of each person according to the new requirements of civilized society in the XXI century. Apart from the fact this equally addresses previous international disagreements (pages 14-19).

7. Considering that 1.3 billion people starve, special attention needs to be paid to their food supplies. **For the first time, therefore, we authors offer a solution to food security issues: in particular, to the increased productivity of various cultures by applying a revolutionary formula in agriculture.** Interestingly, following 2004 - the Russian academy of natural sciences and Hanover University (Germany) awarded a diploma to us authors for the scientific discoveries discussed in this text. Our award including the work we undertook on the biorhythms of plants, the gravitational fields of the Sun, Moon, Earth (along other planets in our Solar system), and their electromagnetic fields. All boding well for the reception of our invetsigations globally.

    Curiously, these little-known patterns of strengthening the bioresonant activation of crops seem to be aligned to the electromagnetic processes within seeds. As such, crops have a frequency multiple to their biorhythms - during the periods of minimum values of gravitational forces and the maximum intensity of space radiation. Each exhibiting the extent of bioresonant activation in the plants and leading, as it does, to an increase in the speed of germination, productivity, the improvement of quality - along with other indicators of efficiency. Each assertion being experimentally determined (pages 62-87)

8. Our main research scope includes agriculture – cotton, grain crops (wheat, barley, rice, etc.). Moreover, the new technologies successfully passed tests by the Ministry of Agriculture of the RK: the Scientific and

Research Agricultural Institute (by Barayev) and other scientific institutes of our RK. Unsurprisingly, foreign research bodies like JSC "Elite Seeds of Tatarstan", the Chelyabinsk Scientific Research Agricultural Institute (Russia), the Deutshe – Pussisches Institut fuz Biomagnettische Kybernetik und Nanoteshnologie (Germany,Berlin), the Agricultural University (by S. Dimerel - Sparta, Turkey), the scientific research institutes of Uzbekistan, Ukraine, Tajikistan equally commended our work. **Overall, this technology is approved in 6 RK areas and 7 states across the World: everywhere achieving positive results.** An increase in crops from 30-40%, was noted in 11 countries. These crops included wheat, barley, rice, corn, potatoes, etc. Each testifying to the environmental friendliness and adaptability of this technology. Indeed, details of these technologies are published in number of media in our Republic of Kazakhstan. **Obviously, there are acts of implementation, patents, certificates and other documents corresponding to these organizations** (pages 62-133).

9. Our central assertions (being stated in this monograph) across the years having been approved by authors at a number of international congresses, symposiums, conferences, forums et al. Including those held in Shanghai, Beijing, Berlin, Moscow, St. Petersburg, Astana, Almaty, Bishkek, Antalya, Bursa, Sparta, Alushta, Donetsk, Tashkent, Baku, Ashgabat, Kazan, Dushanbe, etc (pages 41,58,134 and others).

10. 10. Lastly, the results considered in this monograph can give a new impulse to the strategic development of humanity in the XXI century -- and especially to the preservation of world safety. Our suggested methods covering the food supply of one billion starving people. Furthermore, there are responses from Nobel Prize winning co-laureates, academicians from the Washington Academy of Sciences (S.A.Timashev), academicians from the Russian Academy of Sciences (B.R.Shchuba, A.I.Tatarkin) and a number of famous scientists in foreign or neighbouring countries.

About the Authors

Orazaly Sabden, born May 20th, 1947, in the village of Tastumsyk in the Tyulkubassk district of South Kazakhstan region, Kazakh SSR.

He graduated from the Kazakh Institute of Chemical Technology (1970). Doctor of Economics (1989). Professor (1999), Academician of the MIA and NIARK (1992), the Academy of Sciences of the Republic of Kazakhstan and VSHIHEAS(1996), Academician of the IEA"Eurasia"(1998), akademik Kazakhstan National Academy of Natural Sciences(2009), President of the Republican Public Union-tion "Union of Scientists" (2006).

1970 – 1973 period. – Workedat (the) Shymkent - leading plant in the trust "Kazmontazhavtomatika."

1973 – 1990 period. - Senior Economist: junior, senior, chief researcher at the Institute of Economics of Kazakhstan.

1990 – 2001 period. - Elected a deputy of the Republic of Kazakhstans Parlament. Also, Chairman of the Committee on Economic Reform ….. on the development of science and public education.

2001 – 2003 period. - President of the International Kazakh-Turic University. HAYasavi.

Years 2004 - 2006. – Professor KazATC named Tynyshpayev, President of the Institute for the Analysis and Forecasting regarding "Kazakhstan -United States."

2006 – 2012 period. - Director of the Institute of Economics of the MES.

Since 2012 - Head of Research Center, Senior Researcher, Institute of Economy MES.

Author of over 600 scientific publications, including 70 monographs. In the context of international integration of science and education, he attaches great importance to international cooperation with leading foreign scientific and educational centers in the United States, China, Turkey, EU, CIS etc, adequately representing the economics of Kazakhstan abroad. As one of the leaders of the Standing Committee on Science and Education, Culture and Media of the International Assembly of CIS countries, he has made a significant contribution to ensure the legislative reform of the economic system in CIS countries.

A Member of the Scientific Council on complex problems of Eurasian economic integration, modernization, competitiveness and sustainable development. A body established by order of the President of the Russian Academy of Sciences (№ 296from18.09.2012). Also, a member of the new technologies of the EurAsEC (since 2010), and an actual member of the International Academy of Engineering, the International Academy of higher Education and the International Academy of Innovation.

Currently, developing five major international projects:

1. Creating a new spiritual and technological cluster "Turkestan Valley", which has no analogues in the world.
2. Developing a method for determining a single, universal measurement currency for the entire world in the form of "power", ie. E. RatiokW/ currency.
3. Evolving a new global ideological model of world order.
4. Examining the humanization of society and security- the basis of a new world order.
5. Designing strategies for the survival of humankind in the XXI century and the next.

Master of Sports of the USSR in free style wrestling as a Kazakh champion.
Equally, he is the author of the idea of the album "A Panoramic History of Turkic peoples" (2003), as well as caring for the historical monument

"Tyrkibasy Əuliesi" (2004), built at his own expense. The author is scripting a feature films "Broken Feeling" (2007), "A Good Man" (2014)

A winner of the Lenin Komsomol Prize in the field of science and technology (1980), he also won the State Prize in Republic of Kazakhstan in the fields of science, technology and education (2003). Indeed, his outstanding achievements in the field of strengthening scientific collaboration between Russia and Kazakhstan in 2007, as well as the Russian Security Council, were recongized by his award of the the Order of the MV University. Medalhasan outstanding scientist V. I. Vernadsky.

Abdumalik Ashirov was born in Tashkent on 1 March 1944, into a family of teachers. After graduating from high school - starting in 1961 until 1967 - he studied at the physico-chemical faculty of the Moscow Chemical-Technological Institute named after D.I. Mendeleev.

He began his career in 1967 at the Kazakh Chemical-Technological Institute as an engineer of the laboratory.

From 1968 to 1980, after finishing graduate school, he worked as a senior lecturer, senior researcher and Assistant Professor for the Physical and Colloid Chemistry Department.

In 1973, he defended his thesis.

In 1980, he was appointed as a head of the problematic laboratory at KazHTI. In 1992, he defended his doctoral thesis «Investigation of absorption and hydrogenation of monosaccharides in order to produce poluatomic spirts».

From 1992 to 1994, he worked in the department of the Shymkent International Kazakh-Turkish University (IKTU) named after H.A.Yasavi as a head of the department, Dean of the faculty and Vice-Rector.

From 1994 to 1998, he worked as the Rector of the Tashkent branch (Tashkent Pedagogical Institute) IKTU named after Yasavi; since 1998 – Advisor to the President of the IKTU named after Yasavi. Since 2000 – Head of the Department of General Chemistry.

From 2004 to 2008 – Director of the Institute of Ecology of IKTU named after Yasavi.

From 2008 to 2012 – the Rector of the University of «Sirdarya». From 2012 to the presend A.Ashirov has served as President of the University of «Sirdarya».

A leading expert in the field of heterogeneous catalysis and biotechnology, he is also the author of more than 50 patents and copyright certificates on various inventions: more than 250 scientific articles, 11 monographs and textbooks. Under the guidance of Professor Ashirov 3 doctoral and 16 master's theses were defended. The results of his research being used in productions in Uzbekistan, Kazakhstan, Tajikistan, Russia, Ukraine, Turkey and Germany. He was awarded a medal "For contributing to the development of science in the Republic of Kazakhstan."

Additionall, Professor Ashirov was chosen as the «Best Inventor» of 2001-2005 in a dicision by the National Innovation Fund, the Ministry of Industry and Trade of the Republic of Kazakhstan and the Association of Universities of Kazakhstan. In 2004, after an examination by Russia and Germany in Hannover, he was awarded a diploma for scientific discovery № 272 under the name «The pattern of amplification of bio-resonance activation for seed crops» and the medal of Nobel laureate P.L. Kapitsa as the «Author of scientific discovery».

Titles list

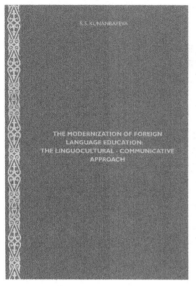

The Modernization of Foreign Language Education: The Linguocultural - Communicative Approach
by SalimaKunanbayeva (2013)

Professor S. S. Kunanbayeva - Rector of Ablai Khan Kazakh University of International Relations and World Languages This textbook is the first of its kind in Kazakhstan to be devoted to the theory and practice of foreign language education. It has been written primarily for future teachers of foreign languages and in a wider sense for all those who to be interested in the question (in the problems?) of the study and use of foreign languages. This book outlines an integrated theory of modern foreign language learning (FLL) which has been drawn up and approved under the auspices of the school of science and methodology of Kazakhstan's Ablai Khan University of International Relations and World Languages.

PAPERBACK
ISBN: **978-0957480780**
RRP: **£19.95**
AVAILABLE ON **KINDLE**

Kairat Zakiryanov

Under the Wolf nest.
Turkic Rhapsody

Көкжал белгісімен. Түркі рапсодиясы

Under Wolf's Nest
by KairatZakiryanov
English –Kazakh edition

Were the origins of Islam, Christianity and the legend of King Arthur all influenced by steppe nomads from Kazakhstan? Ranging through thousands of years of history, and drawing on sources from Herodotus through to contemporary Kazakh and Russian research, the crucial role in the creation of modern civilisation played by the Turkic people is revealed in this detailed yet highly accessible work. Professor Kairat Zakiryanov, President of the Kazakh Academy of Sport and Tourism, explains how generations of steppe nomads, including Genghis Khan, have helped shape the language, culture and populations of Asia, Europe, the Middle East and America through migrations taking place over millennia.

HARD BACK
ISBN: **9780957480728**
RRP: **£17.50**
AVAILABLE ON **KINDLE**

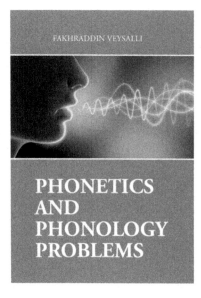

Phonetics and Phonology Problems
by Fahraddin Veysalli

In this manual, the phonetic structure of the Azerbaijani language and its phonological systems have been (systematically) explained by focusing on comparative materials from a number of different languages. Thus, the author defends his theoretical position, as well as persues common principles, through the topics raised. Additionally, he demonstrates his thoughts and considerations, while basing his own investigations upon existing perceptions in literature. As such, this book is primarily intended for philologists. However, these materials can be used by teachers of language or literature, along with postgraduates, dissertants, and students of philological faculties: including everyone interested in linguistics.

PAPER BACK
ISBN: **9781910886182**
RRP: **£19.95**